AP PHYSICS B
CRASH COURSE™

CAMILLA STEJSKAL

By Rebecca Howell, M.Ed.

Research & Education Association
Visit our website at: www.rea.com

Research & Education Association
61 Ethel Road West
Piscataway, New Jersey 08854
E-mail: info@rea.com

AP PHYSICS B CRASH COURSE

Published 2014
Copyright © 2012 by Research & Education Association, Inc.
All rights reserved. No part of this book may be reproduced in any form without permission of the publisher.

Printed in the United States of America

Library of Congress Control Number 2011942460

ISBN-13: 978-0-7386-0934-8
ISBN-10: 0-7386-0934-X

AP PHYSICS B CRASH COURSE TABLE OF CONTENTS

PART I — INTRODUCTION

PART II — MECHANICS

PART III — FLUID MECHANICS, KINETIC THEORY, AND THERMODYNAMICS

PART IV — ELECTRICITY AND MAGNETISM

PART V — WAVES AND OPTICS

PART VI — MODERN PHYSICS

PART VII — THE EXAM

ONLINE PRACTICE EXAM........... *www.rea.com/studycenter*

ABOUT THIS BOOK

This *AP Physics B Crash Course* is the first book of its kind for the last-minute studier or any AP student who wants a quick refresher on the course. REA's *Crash Course* is based on a careful analysis of the AP Physics B Course Description outline and actual AP test questions.

Written by an AP Physics B expert, our easy-to-read format gives students a crash course in the basic knowledge of physics, including theories and techniques, concepts, and general principles. The targeted review chapters prepare students for the exam by focusing only on the topics tested on the AP Physics B exam.

Part One, the introduction, discusses the keys for success and shows you strategies to help you build your overall point score. Part Two is an overview of mechanics and covers Newton's laws of motion and force, circular motion, momentum, and work and energy. In Part Three, the author highlights information on fluid mechanics, kinetic theory, and thermodynamics. Part Four is devoted to electricity and magnetism, and Part Five covers waves and optics. Part Six closes out the content review with a chapter devoted to modern physics.

Part Seven gives you general AP test-taking strategies and teaches you how to master the multiple-choice and free-response sections of the exam. A chapter on essential equations is also included for added study.

No matter how or when you prepare for the AP Physics B exam, REA's *Crash Course* will show you how to study efficiently and strategically, so you'll be ready for the exam.

To check your test readiness for the AP Physics B exam, either before or after studying this *Crash Course*, take REA's **FREE online practice exam**. To access your practice exam, visit the online REA Study Center at *www.rea.com/studycenter* and follow the on-screen instructions. This true-to-format test features automatic scoring, detailed explanations of all answers, and diagnostic score reporting that will help you identify your strengths and weaknesses so you'll be ready on exam day!

Good luck on your AP Physics B exam!

ABOUT OUR AUTHOR

Rebecca Howell has eleven years of experience as an AP Physics B and AP Physics C teacher. She has taught all levels of high school physics, astronomy, and meteorology. She is currently teaching AP Physics B and AP Physics C at Alpharetta High School, Alpharetta, Georgia.

Ms. Howell received her B.S.Ed. in Secondary Science Education—specializing in Physics—from the University of Georgia in Athens, Georgia and earned her M.Ed. in Secondary Science Education at Georgia State University, Atlanta, Georgia.

In addition to her work in the classroom, she has served as an AP Physics B question author, reviewer, Reader and Table Leader for ETS and the College Board for eight years. Ms. Howell was an invited presenter at the Annual Georgia Department of Education AP Workshop. She is also a member of the American Association of Physics Teachers.

AUTHOR ACKNOWLEDGMENTS

I would like to thank Bill Pappas for his invaluable review and commentary of my manuscript and Jeff Funkhouser for his endless support and encouragement during the course of writing this book. I would also like to extend special thanks to my husband, Michael, and my daughter, Olivia, for giving me the time I needed to complete this project.

—*Rebecca Howell*

REA ACKNOWLEDGMENTS

In addition to our author, we would like to thank Larry B. Kling, Vice President, Editorial, for his overall guidance, which brought this publication to completion; Pam Weston, Publisher, for setting the quality standards for production integrity and managing the publication to completion; Diane Goldschmidt, Senior Editor, for editorial project management; Alice Leonard and Kathleen Casey, Senior Editors, for preflight editorial review; and Weymouth Design, for designing our cover.

We also extend our special thanks to William Pappas for his technical review of the manuscript, Marianne L'Abbate for copyediting, and Kathy Caratozzolo of Caragraphics for typesetting this edition.

PART I
INTRODUCTION

Keys for Success
on the AP Physics B Exam

Taking any Advanced Placement exam can be a daunting experience. The AP Physics B exam is no exception. After all, the exam is based on a college-level introductory physics course, and you're still in high school! Don't panic . . . relax. This *Crash Course* is going to guide you to success on the exam.

The AP Physics B course and exam require you to develop your critical-thinking skills, along with developing an in-depth understanding of the discipline of physics, including theories and techniques, concepts, and general principles of the subject.

Our *Crash Course* was designed to help you be more pragmatic in your approach to studying for the AP Physics B exam—in a streamlined outline format.

1. Understand the Structure of the Exam

The AP Physics B exam consists of both multiple-choice questions as well as free-response questions. The sections of the exam are presented as follows:

	Number of Questions/ Problems	Time (minutes)	
Section I			
Multiple-choice questions	70	90	no calc
Section II			
Free-response questions	6 or 7	90	calc
TOTAL TIME		180	

Section I, the multiple-choice section of the exam, is worth 50 percent of your score. Section II, the free-response section, represents the remaining 50 percent of your score. The multiple-choice answers are scored electronically, and you are not penalized for incorrect answers. Therefore, it makes sense to guess if you don't know an answer.

Using Calculators on the AP Physics B Exam

Calculators cannot be used on the multiple-choice section of the AP Physics B exam. However, you may use a graphing or programmable calculator during the free-response section. Visit the College Board website (*www.collegeboard.org*) for more information on what calculators are allowed.

2. Understand the AP Physics B Topical Outline

Many students believe that members of the AP Physics B exam development committee have the freedom to write any question they wish. This is not true. AP Physics B test writers use a detailed topical outline that tells them what they can ask and what they cannot ask.

Every question on the AP Physics B exam can be linked to a specific point in the topical outline. The approximate percentages of questions devoted to each major category that you'll find on the exam are also noted. Familiarize yourself with this outline before studying for the exam and you'll know where to focus your study time. The major topics found on the Physics B exam are:

    I.   Newtonian Mechanics (35%)

        A. Kinematics

        B. Newton's Laws of Motion

        C. Work, Energy, Power

        D. Systems of Particles, Linear Momentum

        E. Circular Motion and Rotation

        F. Oscillations and Gravitation

    II. Fluid Mechanics and Thermal Physics (15%)

        A. Fluid Mechanics

   B. Temperature and Heat

   C. Kinetic Theory and Thermodynamics

III. Electricity and Magnetism (25%)

   A. Electrostatics

   B. Conductors, Capacitors, Dielectrics

   C. Electric Circuits

   D. Magnetic Fields

   E. Electromagnetism

IV. Waves and Optics (15%)

   A. Wave Motion

   B. Physical Optics

   C. Geometric Optics

V. Atomic and Nuclear Physics (10%)

   A. Atomic Physics and Quantum Effects

   B. Nuclear Physics

3. Understand How the Exam Is Scored

The College Board reports your combined multiple-choice score and your total free-response score or a five-point scale:

5	Extremely well-qualified
4	Well-qualified
3	Qualified
2	Possibly qualified
1	No recommendation

Many colleges give course credit with a score of 3 or better; other colleges take nothing below a 4, while still others give college credit only for the top score, a 5. Find out the AP policies of the colleges to which you are seeking admission. Also, be aware that colleges and universities can change their AP acceptance policies whenever they want.

2011 AP Physics B Grade Distributions

Exam Grade	Number of Test Takers Achieving Score	Percent of Test Takers Receiving Score
5	12,369	16.4
4	14,522	19.2
3	19,598	25.9
2	13,065	17.3
1	16,094	21.3
Total Students Earning a 3 or Higher	46,489	61.5

(*Source:* College Board, 2011)

While it is interesting to see what percentage of people scored at each grade for this test—and these numbers are pretty standard from year to year—it should have little impact on how you do on the exam. If you study for the test using our *AP Physics B Crash Course* and pay attention during the school year, you will likely be pleased when you receive your score.

4. Understand the Overlap Between the Multiple-Choice Questions and the Free-Response Questions

Both the multiple-choice questions and the free-response question are taken from the topical outline in the *Course Description Booklet*. As a result, studying for the multiple-choice questions is tantamount to studying for the free-response questions. Many students fail to grasp the significance of this point. Since the multiple-choice questions are highly predictable, so are the free-response questions. The two types of questions are, in fact, highly related, since they both come from the same topical outline.

5. Know Some Basic Test-Taking Strategies

Keep in mind that one of the best ways to prepare for this exam is to take the AP Physics B Practice Exam available online with the purchase of this book. This practice exam will help you become familiar with the format of the test and the types of questions you will be asked. The Detailed Explanations of Answers section will provide feedback that will help you to understand which questions gave you the most difficulty. Then you can go back to the text of this book, reread the appropriate sections of your textbook, or ask your teacher for help. For additional practice tests, check the College Board (*www.collegeboard.org*) website for released past exams. The more questions you answer in preparation for this test, the better you will do on the actual exam.

When it comes time to take the actual test, remember to read all the questions carefully, and be alert for words like "always," "never," "not," and "except." On the multiple-choice section, review all the answer choices before selecting your answer.

On the free-response section, make sure you write clearly. This sounds like a very simple thing, but if those who are scoring your exam cannot read your answer, you will not get credit. You should cross out any errors—using a single line through any mistakes—rather than erase them.

Also on the free-response section, pay particular attention to questions that use the words "justify," "explain," "calculate," "determine," "derive," "sketch," and "plot." All of these words have precise meanings. Pay attention to these words and answer the question asked in order to receive maximum credit. Avoid including irrelevant or extraneous material in your answer.

At this stage of your school career, it is probably too obvious to remind you of some basic preparations right before test day—but we will anyway: get a good night's sleep the night before the exam, eat a good breakfast, and don't forget a bunch of those famous No. 2 pencils.

6. Use College Board and REA Materials to Supplement Your *Crash Course*

This *Crash Course* contains everything you need to know to score well on the AP Physics B exam. You should, however, supplement it with materials provided by the College Board, especially the *AP Physics Course Description Booklet*. The College Board's AP Central website contains a wealth of material to help you prepare for the exam. In addition, REA's *AP Physics B&C* test preparation guide contains excellent narrative chapters that supplement the *Crash Course* chapters.

PART II

MECHANICS

Motion

Chapter

I. LINEAR MOTION

A. *Linear motion* is defined as the motion of an object that is moving in only one dimension, either the *x* or the *y* direction.

1. The linear motion quantities can be defined as either *vectors* or *scalars*.

   i. *Vectors* are quantities that describe both the magnitude (size) and direction of a measurement.

   ii. *Scalars* are quantities that describe only the magnitude of the measurement.

2. Three measurements are used to describe linear motion:

   i. Time, *t*, is a scalar quantity measured by a clock. Time is measured in seconds, *s*.

   ii. Distance, *d*, is a scalar quantity that describes how far an object moved. Distance is measured in meters, *m*.

   iii. Displacement (or "change in position"), Δx, is a vector quantity that describes the change in position of the object or how far and in what direction an object moved; measured in meter, *m*.

3. Putting the basic measurements of time and distance or time and displacement together yields quantities that describe the motion of the object.

   i. Speed, *v*, is a scalar quantity that describes the distance covered per time unit and measured in $\frac{\text{meters}}{\text{second}}\left(\frac{\text{m}}{\text{s}}\right)$.

ii. Velocity, $\vec{v}$, is a vector quantity that describes the change in position per change in time with the direction; measured in $\dfrac{\text{meters}}{\text{second}}$ $\left(\dfrac{m}{s}\right)$.

iii. Acceleration, a, is a vector quantity that describes the change in velocity per change in time with direction, measured in $\dfrac{\text{meters}}{\text{second}^2}$ $\left(\dfrac{m}{s^2}\right)$.

Test Tip

The symbol v is used for speed and velocity; however, it is important to understand the difference in speed and velocity, as the direction is essential for equations that require velocity.

4. Calculating the slope of the straight line on a graph of distance vs. time, shown in Figure 2.1 below, gives the speed, v, of the object.

$$v = \frac{\Delta d}{\Delta t} = \frac{d_2 - d_1}{t_2 - t_1}$$

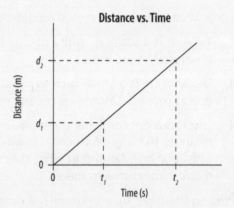

Figure 2.1

5. Calculating the slope of the straight line on a graph of position vs. time, as shown in Figure 2.2 below, gives the velocity, $\vec{v}$, of the object.

$$\vec{v} = \frac{\Delta x}{\Delta t} = \frac{x_2 - x_1}{t_2 - t_1}$$

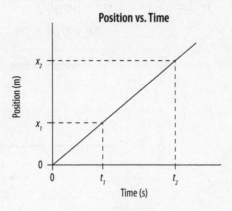

Figure 2.2

6. Calculating the slope of the straight line on a graph of velocity vs. time, as shown in Figure 2.3 below, gives the acceleration, a, of the object.

$$a = \frac{\Delta v}{\Delta t} = \frac{v_2 - v_1}{t_2 - t_1}$$

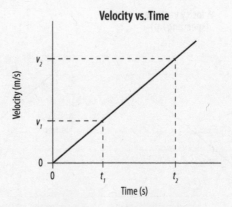

Figure 2.3

7. Calculating the area under the straight line on a graph of velocity vs. time, as shown in Figure 2.4 below, gives the change in position, Δx.

    i.   Figure 2.4 shows the change in position of an object moving at a constant velocity. The area is represented by the shaded section, which is simply the area of a rectangle (A = base × height).

$$\Delta x = \text{area} = vt$$

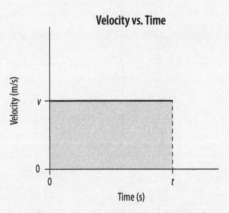

Figure 2.4

    ii.   Figure 2.5(a) shows the change in position of an object speeding up and Figure 2.5(b) shows the change in position of an object slowing down.

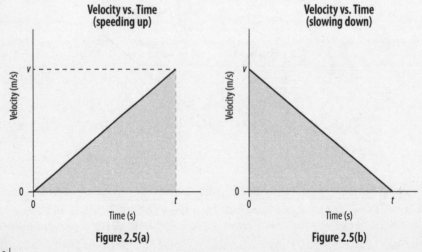

Figure 2.5(a)   Figure 2.5(b)

iii. The change in position, Δx, in Figure 2.5a and Figure 2.5b, is the area of the shaded section, which is simply the area of a triangle ($A = \dfrac{1}{2}$ base × height).

$$\Delta x = \text{area} = \frac{1}{2} vt$$

8. The three basic equations for motion can be derived from the velocity vs. time graph. These three equations will be on the AP Physics B Equation Sheet.

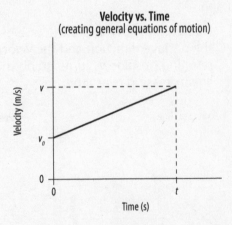

Velocity vs. Time
(creating general equations of motion)

Figure 2.6

i. The straight line on the velocity time graph, shown above in Figure 2.6, is $v = v_o + at$.

ii. The equation for the area under the graph above, is

$$\Delta x = v_o t + \frac{1}{2} at^2$$

iii. Combining the two equations above to eliminate t results in $v^2 = v_o^2 = 2a\Delta x$.

The AP Physics B Equation sheet uses $x - x_o$ for Δx.

9. Constant velocity implies zero acceleration. In which case, $v = v_o$.

   i. If the velocity does not change, the change in position (as shown in Figure 2.4) is $\Delta x = v_o t$.

   ii. The change in position, or displacement, is proportional to the speed and time.

10. When an object is accelerating, the velocity is changing, which means the rate at which the position changes is also affected. In the figures below, a general velocity vs. time graph is shown with its corresponding position vs. time graph.

    i. Figure 2.7 below shows the case of an object moving in the positive direction and the velocity increasing. The resulting position vs. time graph shows the slope of the line increasing over time.

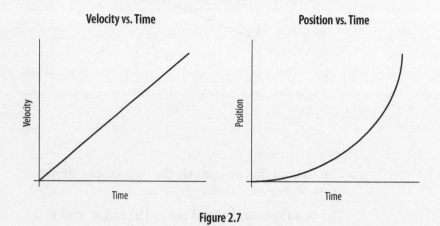

Velocity vs. Time   **Position vs. Time**

Figure 2.7

Note: Since the initial velocity is zero, the initial slope of the position vs. time curve is zero. However, as the velocity increases, the slope of the position vs. time curve increases.

ii. Figure 2.8 below shows the case of an object moving in the positive direction and the velocity decreasing. The resulting position vs. time graph shows the slope of the line decreasing over time.

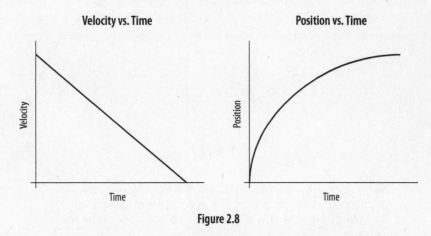

Figure 2.8

Note: Since the initial velocity is greater than zero, the initial slope of the position vs. time curve is greater than zero. However, as the velocity decreases, the slope of the line approaches zero.

iii. Figure 2.9 below shows the case of an object moving in the negative direction and the magnitude of the velocity increasing. The resulting position vs. time graph shows the absolute value of the slope of the line increasing (in the negative direction) over time.

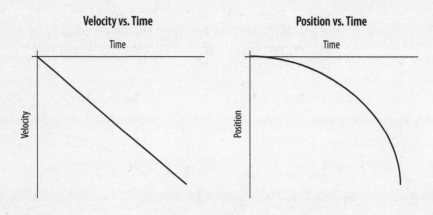

Figure 2.9

Note: Since the initial velocity is zero, the initial slope of the position vs. time curve is zero. However, as the magnitude of the velocity increases, the absolute value of the slope of the line increases.

iv. Figure 2.10 below shows the case of an object moving in the negative direction and the magnitude of the velocity is decreasing. The resulting position vs. time graph shows the absolute value of the slope of the line decreasing over time.

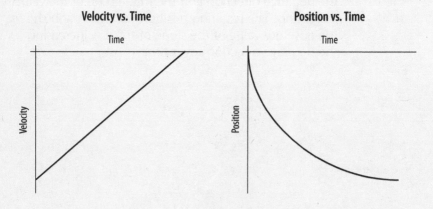

Figure 2.10

Note: Since the magnitude of the initial velocity is greater than zero, the magnitude of the initial slope of the position vs. time curve is greater than zero. However, as the magnitude of the velocity decreases, the absolute value of the slope of the line approaches zero.

Be prepared to read and interpret graphs on the AP Physics exam. Always consider what the slope of the graph yields.

B. *Free-fall motion* is a form of linear motion in one dimension. The acceleration in free fall is due to gravity.

1. The acceleration of an object in free-fall, *g*, represents the acceleration due to gravity

For Earth, $g = 9.8 \dfrac{m}{s^2}$.

It is common for the coordinate system used for free fall to denote down as negative, in which case a negative sign is needed for the acceleration of gravity.

$$v = v_0 - gt$$

$$\Delta y = v_0 t - \frac{1}{2}gt^2$$

$$v^2 = v_0^2 - 2g\,\Delta y$$

2. The three standard equations of motion can be used, with −*g* substituted for *a*.

For the purposes of the AP Physics B exam, you are allowed and encouraged to use the approximate value of $g = 10 \dfrac{m}{s^2}$.

3. A graph of the vertical position vs. time of an object thrown straight up is in the shape of a parabola, as shown in Figure 2.11 below. The initial velocity of the object is greater than zero and positive. Immediately, the acceleration due to gravity acts on the object causing it to slow down while moving in the positive direction, until it stops at the highest point. The acceleration due to gravity causes the object to change direction and speed up in the negative direction, falling back to Earth.

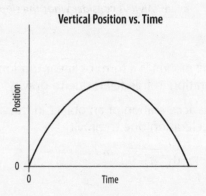

Vertical Position vs. Time

Figure 2.11

Often AP Physics multiple-choice questions will test your ability to match position vs. time graphs to the velocity vs. time graph.

4. The corresponding velocity vs. time and acceleration vs. time graphs are shown below in Figure 2.12. The initial velocity is positive and greater than zero, but the acceleration, or the slope of the velocity vs. time graph, is the acceleration due to gravity, which is negative. Therefore, the shape of the velocity vs. time curve is a straight line with a negative slope. The point where the velocity vs. time curve intersects the time axis corresponds to the time when the object is at the highest point of its path. The velocity vs. time curve then continues in the negative region of the graph which corresponds to the object falling back to the Earth, in the negative direction. The acceleration vs. time

curve is a straight line representing the constant value, $a = g$ $= -9.8\frac{m}{s^2}$.

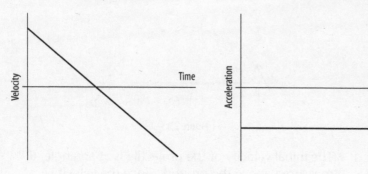

Figure 2.12

5. The acceleration due to gravity is always directed straight down, including when the object stops momentarily at the highest point of the motion.

Test Tip

In free-fall problems, the acceleration due to gravity is not stated explicitly within the text of the problem. It is assumed to be understood.

II. PROJECTILE MOTION

A. *Projectile motion* is motion that occurs in two dimensions simultaneously, the *x* and *y* directions.

B. In ideal projectile motion, the only acceleration the object experiences is the acceleration due to gravity, $9.8\frac{m}{s^2}$. The path of a projectile is called a *trajectory* and is in the shape of a parabola.

1. The most traditional type of projection is "ground to ground," as shown in Figure 2.13 below.

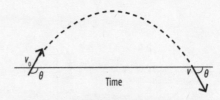

Trajectory of a Projectile
(ground to ground)

Figure 2.13

i. The initial velocity of the projectile is at an angle, θ, measured above the ground. Since the velocity is at an angle, it has an x and a y component. Therefore, the velocity must be mathematically separated into its components.

$$v_{ox} = v_o\cos\theta$$

$$v_{oy} = v_o\sin\theta$$

For a "ground to ground" projection, the magnitude of the final velocity is equal in magnitude and opposite in direction of the initial velocity.

ii. The acceleration in the x direction is zero, which means the velocity in the x direction does not change during the projection. So, $v_{ox} = v_x$.

iii. The acceleration in the y direction is due to gravity, which means the velocity in the y direction changes during the projection.

$$v_y = -v_o\sin\theta - gt$$

For a "ground to ground" projection, the final velocity in the y direction is equal and opposite to the initial velocity in the y direction.

iv. The three basic equations for motion can be applied, but the *x* and *y* values must be treated separately. The equations shown below have been manipulated to apply to the specific component direction.

x direction	*y* direction
$\Delta x = v_{ox}t$	$v_y = v_{oy} - gt$ $\Delta y = v_{oy}t - \dfrac{1}{2}gt^2$ $v_y^2 = v_{oy}^2 - 2g\Delta y$

v. Time is the only variable that can be used in both dimensions. The object moves in the *x* and *y* directions during the same amount of time.

For a "ground to ground" projection, the object reaches the highest point at half the total time. The velocity in the y direction is zero and the velocity in the x direction is $v_x = v_o cos\theta$.

2. Another common type of projection is a "horizontal" projection, as shown in Figure 2.14 below. The path, as shown, is half of a parabola.

"Horizontal" Projectile Trajectory

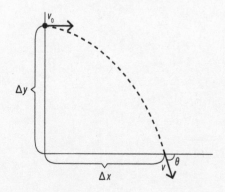

Figure 2.14

Test Tip *The horizontal projection is one of the most common types of projectile motion problems found on the AP Physics exam.*

i. The initial velocity is the initial velocity in the x direction, $v_o = v_{ox}$, and since the acceleration in the x direction is zero, the final velocity in the x direction is the initial velocity, $v_o = v_o$.

ii. The initial velocity in the y direction is zero, it is not moving up or down as it is projected in the x direction.

iii. When the object lands, it is moving in both the x and y directions, thus the final velocity is the result of the two components.

$$v_R = \sqrt{v_x^2 + v_y^2}$$

$$v_x = v_o \text{ and } v_y = -gt$$

iv. And the direction of the velocity is $\theta = \tan^{-1}\dfrac{v_y}{v_x}$.

Test Tip *Since the velocity in the y direction is zero, the position equation reduces to $\Delta y = -\dfrac{1}{2}gt^2$, which makes finding the height or the time a simple calculation.*

Newton's Laws of Motion and Force

I. NEWTON'S LAWS

A. Newton's First Law of Motion (N1L): An object at rest stays at rest, an object in motion stays in motion, unless acted on by an unbalanced force.

1. N1L is also known as the "Law of Inertia": the tendency of an object to resist change.

2. N1L describes objects in equilibrium. Equilibrium implies that the acceleration is zero and that the forces are balanced.

3. The equation form of N1L is:

   $$\Sigma F = 0$$

Test Tip *A zero or constant velocity means the acceleration is zero, and the forces are balanced and vice versa: when the forces are balanced, the acceleration is zero.*

B. Newton's Second Law of Motion (N2L): When a net force acts on an object, it will accelerate at a rate that is proportional to the force but inversely proportional to the mass of the object.

1. The net force is the vector sum of all the forces acting in the x and y directions

2. The equation form of N2L is

$$\Sigma F_x = ma_x$$

and

$$\Sigma F_y = ma_y$$

C. Newton's Third Law of Motion (N3L): For every force there is a force that is equal in magnitude and opposite in direction between two bodies.

1. These are called action/reaction forces and can be seen as pairs of forces on two bodies.

2. The equation form of N3L is:

$$F_1 = -F_2$$

Test Tip

The force a mass M applies to mass m is equal and opposite in direction according to N3L. The force does not depend on the masses. The acceleration of the smaller mass is greater than the acceleration of the larger mass.

II. FORCES

A. A force is a vector quantity that describes a push or a pull, measured in newtons (N).

B. Types of forces

1. Weight—*mg*, the force of gravity on an object, directed towards the center of the earth.

weight = *mg*

2. Normal—*n*, the force applied by a surface onto an object, directed perpendicularly to the surface.

3. Tension—*T*, the force in a rope, cord, string, or any other connecting material. The direction of tension can be determined by starting on the object and tracing the cord.

4. Spring force—F_s, the force applied by a spring:

$$F_s = -kx$$

  i. *k* represents the spring constant

  ii. *x* represents the displacement of the spring from equilibrium.

The negative sign in front of the equation is to correct for the direction of the force. The sign for the direction of the displacement must be included in the calculation. A spring always pushes or pulls towards the equilibrium position.

5. Friction—*f*, a resistive force caused by interactions between the surfaces.

$$f = \mu n$$

➤ μ (mu) is the Greek letter used to represent the *coefficient of friction* between the surfaces.

➤ *n* is the normal force, *N*.

The magnitude of μ represents the amount of friction between the two surfaces, a higher μ means the surfaces are rough. μ has no units.

6. Static friction is the friction force between two surfaces when the objects do not move relative to one another. The static friction force ranges from 0 to a maximum value, calculated with $f = \mu_s n$.

7. Kinetic friction is the sliding friction force between two surfaces when the objects move relative to one another. The kinetic friction force is a set value calculated with $f = \mu_k n$.

The greater the normal force, the greater the friction between the surfaces.

C. A "Free-Body Diagram" (FBD) or "Force Diagram" is used to solve complex force problems. Because a force is a vector, it has magnitude and direction. The *x* and *y* components must be separated.

1. An FBD is drawn to indicate the relative size and direction of all the forces acting on a single body. A vector is represented by an arrow.

2. The sum the forces in the *x* and *y* directions creates the force equations for the specific problem.

3. Only the forces ON the chosen object are drawn. Do not include forces exerted BY the object.

D. The table below shows several common situations in which an FBD is needed and the corresponding sum of forces.

1. For horizontal motion, set the *x* axis to be along the horizontal; this will be the direction of the acceleration.

FBD on a Horizontal Plane

Situation	FBD	Force Equations
Sliding to the right, with friction, slowing down	Sliding to the right with friction n $f \leftarrow \square \rightarrow$ mg	$\Sigma F_x = -f = ma$ $\Sigma F_y = n - mg = 0$
Sliding to the right, with a constant velocity	Moving to the right at a constant velocity n $f \leftarrow \square \rightarrow F$ mg	$\Sigma F_x = F - f = 0$ $\Sigma F_y = n - mg = 0$

Situation	FBD	Force Equations
Sliding to the right, speeding up	Moving to the right, accelerating n $f \leftarrow \boxed{m_1} \xrightarrow{F}$ mg	$\Sigma F_x = F - f = ma$ $\Sigma F_y = n - mg = 0$
Sliding to the right, Force inclined at an angle above the surface	n $f \leftarrow \boxed{m_1} \, \nearrow^{F} \theta$ mg	$\Sigma F_x = F \cos\theta - f = ma$ $\Sigma F_y = n + F \sin\theta - mg = 0$

Test Tip *Friction is shown in many of the FBDs shown. If the surface is frictionless, the friction vector can simply be omitted from the FBD.*

2. For vertical motion, set the y axis to be in the vertical direction, this will be the direction of the acceleration.

FBD in Vertical Direction

Situation	FBD	Force Equations
Vertical Equilibrium, with Tension	T $\uparrow$ $\boxed{}$ $\downarrow$ mg	$\Sigma F_x = 0$ $\Sigma F_y = T - mg = 0$
Vertical Acceleration, with Tension	T $\uparrow$ $\boxed{}$ $\downarrow$ mg	$\Sigma F_x = 0$ $\Sigma F_y = T - mg = ma$

3. For the inclined plane, set the *x* axis to be along the plane and the *y* axis to be perpendicular to the plane. The acceleration will be along the plane

 i. Rotate the coordinate axis such that the *x* axis is parallel to the incline plane for objects on an inclined plane.

 ii. The angle of the inclined plane is the same angle between the weight (mg) and the line of the normal force.

FBD on an Inclined Plane

Situation	FBD	Force Equations
Sliding down inclined plane, no friction		$\Sigma F_x = mg \sin \theta = ma$ $\Sigma F_y = n - mg \cos \theta = 0$
Sliding down incline, with friction		$\Sigma F_x = mg \sin \theta - f = ma$ $\Sigma F_y = n - mg \cos \theta = 0$

Test Tip

The spring force, F_s, can be substituted for any of the T forces in the FBD shown.

4. A two-body system (or more) requires two FBD.

 i. Choose a direction for the system to accelerate.

 ii. Draw the FBD for each object.

 iii. Sum the forces acting on each object, taking into account the direction of the acceleration.

FBD of Two Body Systems

Situation	FBD	Force Equations
m_1 is connected to m_2 by a string that passes over a pulley. The surface has friction. $m_2 > m_1$	n up; $f \leftarrow m_1 \rightarrow T$; $m_1 g$ down	$\Sigma F_x = T - f = m_1 a$ $\Sigma F_y = n - m_1 g = 0$
	T up; m_2; $m_2 g$ down	$\Sigma F_x = 0$ $\Sigma F_y = T - m_2 g = -m_2 a$
m_1 is connected to m_2 by a string that passes over a pulley. The surface has friction and is inclined at an angle . $m_2 > m_1$	n; T; m_1; f; θ; mg	$\Sigma F_x = T - f - mg\sin\theta$ $\quad = + m_1 a$ $\Sigma F_y = n - m_1 g \cos\theta = 0$
	T up; m_2; $m_2 g$ down	$\Sigma F_x = 0$ $\Sigma F_y = T - m_2 g = -m_2 a$

Note: In both cases shown above, m_2 is accelerating downward. The result is a negative net force acting on m_2, which is accounted for in the sum of the forces in the y direction, $m_2 a$.

Test Tip

On the AP Physics exam, only resultant force vectors should be drawn. Component vectors should not be included on the diagrams.

Work and Energy

I. WORK

A. In physics terms, *work* is done when a force (or a component of a force) is applied parallel to the distance an object moves through. Work is a scalar quantity.

1. Work is done only when there is a force, or a component of the force, parallel to the displacement. Figure 4.1 shows the force, *F*, pointing to the right and the displacement, Δx, also to the right.

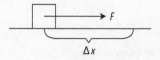

Figure 4.1

➤ The work done is:

$$W = F\Delta x$$

2. Figure 4.2 shows the force, *F*, inclined at an angle, θ, above the horizontal, and the displacement, Δx, to the right.

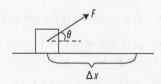

Figure 4.2

➤ The force is at an angle to the displacement, the component of the force, *F cos θ*, is the force that is parallel to the displacement. Therefore, the work done is:

$$W = (F \cos \theta) \Delta x$$

3. Figure 4.3 shows the force, *F*, directed straight up, and the displacement, *Δx*, to the right.

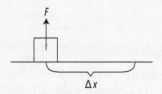

Figure 4.3

➤ The force is directed straight up. There is *no* component of the force parallel to the displacement. The angle between *F* and *Δx* is 90°. Therefore, the work done is:

$$W = 0$$

Test Tip

The work done by a force that is perpendicular to the displacement is always zero (e.g., for an object moving along a surface, the normal force does zero work)

4. The general equation for work is:

$$W = F \Delta x \cos \theta$$

➤ *W* is the work done by the force, *J*

➤ *F* is the magnitude of the force applied, *N*

➤ *Δd* is the displacement the object moves, *m*

➤ *θ* is the angle between the displacement and force, degrees

5. In terms of graphing, work is the *area* under a force vs. displacement graph. In the case where the graph is given, the work is determined by the geometric calculation of the area between the force function and the displacement axis, as shown in Figure 4.4.

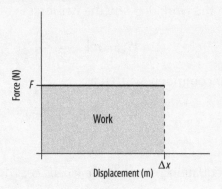

Figure 4.4

Work/Energy concepts can be considered the backbone of most physics problems. Work/Energy can be applied to a variety of problems. Therefore, a solid understanding of work and energy is imperative.

II. WORK-ENERGY THEOREM

A. The net work done on an object is the product of the net force and displacement, Δx.

$$W_{net} = F_{net}\, \Delta x$$

B. When a net force is applied to an object, it accelerates.

$$F_{net} = ma$$

Therefore,

$$W_{net} = ma\, \Delta x$$

From linear motion,

$$v^2 = v_o^2 + 2a\Delta x$$

This means,

$$a\Delta x = \frac{v^2 - v_0^2}{2}$$

Then the work done by the net force is:

$$W_{net} = m\left(\frac{v^2 - v_0^2}{2}\right)$$

More commonly written as:

$$W_{net} = \frac{1}{2}mv^2 - \frac{1}{2}mv_o^2$$

C. The equation, $\frac{1}{2}mv^2$, is the *kinetic energy, K,* of the object. So,

$$W_{net} = K - K_o$$

or

$$W_{net} = \Delta K$$

This is referred to as the *Work-Energy Theorem.*

1. *A good starting place for solving work/energy problems is the* **work-energy theorem,** $W_{net} = \Delta K.$

2. *If an object speeds up, the net work done on it is positive. If the object slows down, the net work done on it is negative.*

3. *If an object is taken from one position at rest and moved to another position at rest, the net work is zero.*

4. *The net work is the same as the work done by the net force, which is equal to the total work done by all of the forces acting on the object.*

III. KINETIC ENERGY

A. Kinetic energy describes the energy of an object that is moving.

B. The kinetic energy is calculated by using:

$$K = \frac{1}{2}mv^2$$

➤ *K* is kinetic energy, J

> ➤ *m* is mass, *kg*

> ➤ *v* is the speed, $\frac{m}{s}$

C. When the kinetic energy changes, net work is done to the object. If the net work done is positive, the kinetic energy increases, if the net work done is negative, the kinetic energy decreases.

Test Tip

The work done by friction is negative. Friction generally takes energy out of a system.

IV. CONSERVATION OF MECHANICAL ENERGY

A. The conservation of energy states that energy cannot be created or destroyed, but it can be transformed from one type to another or transferred from one object to another. *Energy* is the ability to do work.

B. There are two types of forces, *conservative* and *non-conservative*, in nature.

    1. A *conservative force* is one in which the work depends only on the net change in position, not the overall path. The work done by a conservative force is *path independent.*

        i. There are two conservative forces in nature: the gravitational force and the electric force. For purposes of this course, spring force is considered to be conservative for simplification.

    2. A *non-conservative force* is one in which the work depends on the path taken. The work done by a conservative force is *path dependent.*

        i. All forces other than the conservative forces named above are *non-conservative*. Commonly, non-conservative forces will be tension and friction.

C. When the gravitational force, or the weight, is the only force acting on an object, then the work done by that force is:

$$W_{net} = W_g$$

Since $W = F\Delta y$, where Δy is the vertical displacement, the work done by the gravitational force is:

$$W_g = -mg(\Delta y)$$

Here, mg is negative because the gravitational force, weight, is always pointing straight down, towards the center of the planet. The Δy represents the vertical displacement of the object.

Substituting for Δy,

$$W_g = -(mgy - mgy_o)$$

The term mgy is referred to as the *gravitational potential energy*, and given the symbol U.

$$W_g = -(U - U_o)$$

Simplifying gives:

$$W_g = -\Delta U$$

The work done by the gravitational force or any other conservative force is:

$$W_c = \Delta U$$

D. If the gravitational force is the only force doing work on the object, the work done by gravity is the change in kinetic energy.

$$W_g = \Delta K$$

and

$$-\Delta U = \Delta K$$

When expanded, the various forms of this equation, the *Conservation of Mechanical Energy,* are:

$$-(U - U_o) = K - K_o$$

$$K + U = K_o + U_o$$

$$\frac{1}{2}mv^2 + mgy = \frac{1}{2}mv_o^2 + mgy_o$$

V. GRAVITATIONAL POTENTIAL ENERGY

A. Gravitational potential energy, $U = mgy$, represents the amount of energy the object has based on its vertical position relative to a reference height.

1. The energy stored in the position of the object represents the amount of work that can be done on the object by the gravitational force. It is a potential of that conservative force to do work if the object moves in the direction of, or the opposite direction of, that conservative force.

2. As with many scalar quantities, gravitational potential energy can be positive, negative, or zero.

3. *Positive potential energy* implies the object is located above the reference height.

4. *Zero potential energy* means that the object is located at the reference position. However, it does *not* mean that the object has zero energy stored. If the reference height is located at the top of a ramp, an object would lose potential energy if it slid down the ramp.

5. *Negative potential energy* means that the object is located somewhere below the reference height. If an object slides down a ramp from a negative position, the object would move to a more negative position, losing potential energy.

6. Regardless of the reference point for a given problem, the *change* in potential energy should be the same.

more
just then
gravity

B. If other forces, such as tension and friction, are acting on the object, the net work done on the object is the sum of all the work done by each individual force. Then,

$$W_{net} = W_{nc} + W_c$$

➤ W_{nc} is the work done by the *non-conservative force*.

➤ W_c is the work done by the *conservative force*.

If the W_c is the work done by the gravitational force, W_g:

$$W_{net} = W_{nc} - \Delta U$$

Since the $W_{net} = \Delta K$,

$$\Delta K = W_{nc} - \Delta U$$

Then rearranging gives,

$$W_{nc} = \Delta K + \Delta U$$

Additionally, $W_{nc} = \Delta E$,

$$\Delta E = \Delta K + \Delta U$$

In the case where ΔE is zero, mechanical energy is conserved.

$$0 = \Delta K + \Delta U$$

C. The work done by the non-conservative force can be positive or negative, depending on the direction of the force and the displacement.

1. If the non-conservative force is friction, then $W_{nc} = -fd$. The negative sign is important.

2. If the non-conservative force is tension, then $W_{nc} = Td$ if the tension and the displacement are in the same direction. But $W_{nc} = -Td$ if the tension and displacement are in opposite directions.

VI. WORK DONE BY A VARIABLE FORCE, SPRINGS

A. Spring force is a force that is applied to an object by a spring. As before, spring force depends on the spring itself and the displacement by which the spring is stretched or compressed. Just like any other force, spring force does work on an object or the energy can be stored in the stretched/compressed spring.

1. For the purposes of this course, the work done by a spring is considered *conservative*, unless otherwise specified.

2. To calculate the work done by a spring, or the energy stored in a spring, a graph of the spring force vs. displacement can be employed.

3. Figure 4.5 shows a graph of the $|F_s| = |-k\Delta x|$.

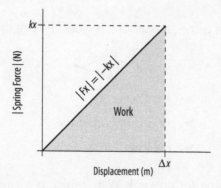

Figure 4.5

The work is the shaded area under the function, which is in the shape of a triangle. Therefore,

$$W_s = \text{area} = \frac{1}{2}bh$$

$$W_s = \frac{1}{2}(x)(kx)$$

$$W_s = \frac{1}{2}kx^2$$

4. The work done on an object is equal to the area under the force vs. displacement graph. The spring force is simplified to a conservative force, and then the absolute value of the work done by the spring is equal to the energy stored in the spring from $W_s = -\Delta U$.

$$W_s = \frac{1}{2}kx^2$$

VII. POWER

A. *Power* is the rate at which work is done or energy is used.

$$P = \frac{W}{t}$$

➤ P is Power, W

➤ W is the work done, J

➤ t is the time, s

B. The unit for power is Watt, which is a joule/second.

C. The $W_{net} = F\Delta x$

$$P = \frac{F\Delta x}{t}$$

And average velocity is:

$$v = \frac{\Delta x}{t}$$

Substitution yields:

$$P = Fv$$

➤ P is power, W

➤ F is the constant force along the direction of the motion, N

➤ v is the average velocity, $\frac{s}{t}$

Test Tip

P = Fv only applies to situations where the force is parallel to the motion and the velocity is constant. If the velocity is changing, then the kinetic energy is changing and the average power can be calculated.

$$P_{avg} = \frac{W}{t} \qquad \Delta \text{velocity}$$

$$P = Fv \qquad \text{Constant velocity}$$

Momentum

I. IMPULSE AND MOMENTUM

A. Impulse and momentum are quantities with roots in Newton's 2nd Law of Motion.

B. A non-zero net force causes an object to accelerate,

$$F_{net} = ma$$

Acceleration means velocity changes over an interval of time.

$$a = \frac{v - v_o}{\Delta t}$$

Then,

$$F_{net} = m\left(\frac{v - v_o}{\Delta t}\right)$$

and

$$F_{net}\Delta t = m(v - v_o)$$

From the equation shown above, the change in velocity depends on the magnitude of the force and the time interval that the force is applied to the object. This concept is called *impulse*.

$$J = F_{net}\Delta t$$

➤ J is impulse, $\frac{kgm}{s}$ or Ns

➤ F_{net} is the net force, N

➤ Δt is the time interval, s

C. The impulse can be determined by calculating the shaded area under the function on a force vs. time graph, as shown in Figure 5.1(a) and (b)

1. Figure 5.1(a) shows the impulse delivered to an object by a constant force.

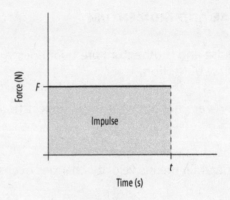

Figure 5.1(a)

➤ The shaded area is a rectangle.

$$J = \text{Area} = bh = Ft$$

2. Figure 5.1(b) shows the impulse delivered to an object by a changing force, as in a collision.

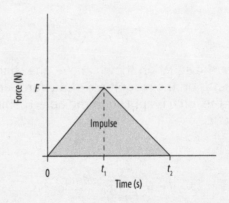

Figure 5.1(b)

➤ The shaded area is a triangle.

$$I = \text{Area} = \frac{1}{2}bh = \frac{1}{2}t_2F$$

3. The impulse causes the velocity to change,

$$J = m(v - v_o)$$

or

$$J = mv - mv_o$$

And the quantity mv is the *momentum* of the object

$$J = p - p_o$$

or

$$J = \Delta p$$

and

$$\Delta p = mv - mv_o$$

i. *Impulse* is a vector quantity that describes the *change in momentum* of an object. Momentum is transferred to the object by a force applied over time. Therefore, momentum is also a vector quantity.

ii. A change in momentum can occur due to a change in the speed of an object or a change in the direction of the velocity, or both.

Test Tip

When an object strikes a wall and bounces off in the opposite direction with the same speed, the momentum of the object has changed because the direction of the velocity has changed.

impulse and momentum
are vectors!

II. CONSERVATION OF MOMENTUM

A. Newton's third law of motion (N3L) states that for every force there is an equal and opposite force between the two objects. Therefore, when two or more objects collide,

$$F_1 = -F_2$$

and they are in contact with one another for the same amount of time, Δt,

$$F_1 \Delta t = -F_2 \Delta t$$

The change in momentum of object 1 is equal and opposite to the change in momentum for object 2.

$$\Delta p_1 = -\Delta p_2$$

Expanding Δp:

$$m_1 v_1 - m_1 v_{10} = (m_2 v_2 - m_2 v_{20})$$

Combining initial and final conditions:

$$m_1 v_{10} + m_2 v_{20} = m_1 v_1 + m_2 v_2$$

which means:

$$p_{10} + p_{20} = p_1 + p_2$$
$$\Sigma p_o = \Sigma p$$

B. Therefore, the total momentum of the system *before* the collision is equal to the total momentum of the system *after* the collision. This is called the *conservation of momentum*. Momentum is conserved in all collisions, provided the contact force between the two objects is the only force present.

III. COLLISIONS

A. There are two types of collisions, inelastic and elastic.

1. In *inelastic collisions*, momentum is conserved and objects are separate before and after the collision.

$$m_1 v_{1o} + m_2 v_{2o} = m_1 v_1 + m_2 v_2$$

i. A special case of an inelastic collision is a perfectly or completely inelastic collision. Momentum is conserved; objects are together *before or after* the collision. The objects "explode" apart or "stick together."

inelastic:
KE is NOT conserved

➤ "explode"—total kinetic energy is greater afterwards.

$$(m_1 + m_2)v_3 = m_1 v_{1o} + m_2 v_{2o}$$

Initially the two objects have a common velocity, v_{3o}

➤ "stick together"—kinetic energy is less afterwards.

$$m_1 v_1 + m_2 v_2 = (m_1 + m_2)v_{3o}$$

Afterward the two objects have a common velocity, v_3.

> *Perfectly inelastic collisions may also be referred to as a "totally" or "completely" inelastic collision.*

> *Often springs are used in perfectly inelastic collisions. The spring's potential energy is converted to kinetic energy. The initial momentum is zero and the final momentum of the system is also zero, as the two objects move in opposite directions.*

2. In *elastic collisions* or perfectly elastic collisions, momentum *and* kinetic energy are conserved.

i. Momentum:

$$m_1 v_{1o} + m_2 v_{2o} = m_1 v_1 + m_2 v_2$$

ii. Kinetic energy:

$$\frac{1}{2}m_1v_{1o}^2 + \frac{1}{2}m_2v_{2o}^2 = \frac{1}{2}m_1v_1^2 + \frac{1}{2}m_2v_2^2$$

iii. The two equations above can be combined, eliminating both *m*'s.

$$v_1 + v_{1o} = v_2 + v_{2o}$$

Often the type of collision is not stated explicitly in a problem, but the conditions of the collision are described. It is best to be comfortable with both the name and the definition of each of the collisions.

B. Glancing collisions are collisions that result in the objects moving in the *x* and *y* directions.

1. Momentum is a vector; therefore, it has *x* and *y* components.

i. When an object collides with a stationary wall and bounces off at an angle, as shown in Figure 5.2, the change in momentum is in the *x* direction only.

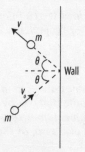

Figure 5.2

➤ the change in momentum in the *x* direction:

$$\Delta p_x = m(-v\cos\theta - v_o\cos\theta)$$

where $v\cos\theta$ is the *x* component of the velocity.

➤ the change in momentum in the *y* direction:

$$\Delta p_y = m(v \sin \theta - v_o \sin \theta)$$

where *v sin θ* is the *y* component of the velocity.

ii. When two objects moving in different directions collide and stick together, as shown in Figure 5.3(a), the resulting momentum is the vector sum of the total momenta, shown in Figure 5.3(b).

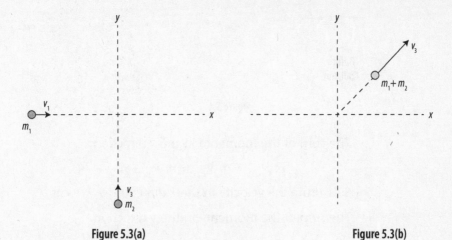

Figure 5.3(a)   Figure 5.3(b)

➤ the initial momentum in the *x* direction:

$$p_{ox} = m_1 v_{o1x}$$

➤ the initial momentum in the *y* direction:

$$p_{oy} = m_2 v_{o2y}$$

➤ the resultant momentum after the collision:

$$p_R = \sqrt{(p_{ox})^2 + (p_{oy})^2}$$

2. Momentum is conserved in both the *x* and *y* directions. The total momentum in both directions is still conserved when objects do not undergo a head-on collision. A glancing collision is shown in Figure 5.4 on the next page.

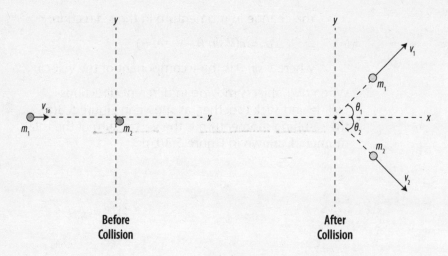

Before Collision

After Collision

Figure 5.4

i. The sum of the momenta in the x direction:

$$m_1 v_{o1x} + m_2 v_{o2x} = m_1 v_{1x} + m_2 v_{2x}$$

Substitute the velocity in the x direction: $v_x = v \cos \theta$

ii. The sum of the momenta in the y direction:

$$m_1 v_{o1y} + m_2 v_{o2y} = m_1 v_{1y} + m_2 v_{2y}$$

Substitute the velocity in the y direction: $v_y = v \sin \theta$

Circular Motion

I. ROTATIONAL MOTION

A. Objects that move in a circular path cover a distance, or arc length, that is related to the radius of the circular path, r, and the angle through which the object has moved through, θ, as shown in Figure 6.1 below.

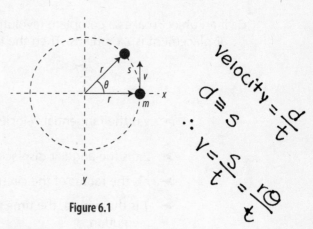

Figure 6.1

$$\boxed{s = r\theta}$$

➤ s is the arc length, m

➤ r is the radius of the circle, m

➤ θ is the angular displacement, radians

B. As the object moves through the arc length, or distance, the velocity can be calculated using:

$$v = \frac{s}{t} = \frac{r\theta}{t}$$

The object's angular displacement per time, $\frac{\theta}{t}$, defines the *angular speed, ω*:

$$\boxed{v = r\omega}$$

➤ *v* is the tangential velocity, $\frac{m}{s}$

➤ *r* is the radius of the circular path, *m*

➤ ω is the angular speed, measured in $\frac{rad}{s}$

Test Tip Angular speed *may also be referred to as* angular velocity.

C. If an object makes a complete revolution, the angular displacement is 2π radians. Then the tangential velocity is:

$$v = \frac{2\pi r}{T}$$

➤ *v* is the tangential velocity, $\frac{m}{s}$

➤ 2π is the angular displacement, radians

➤ *r* is the radius of the circular path, *m*

➤ *T* is the period, the time for one complete revolution, *s*

Test Tip *The two equations for v can be set equal to each other,*
$r\omega = \frac{2\pi r}{T}$.

$$r\omega = \frac{2\pi r}{T}$$

II. CENTRIPETAL FORCE

A. The *centripetal force* is defined as the net force on an object that keeps it moving in a circle.

   1. The centripetal force is not a separate force drawn on a FBD.

   2. The centripetal force is a force that is present on the object, e.g., gravitational force, friction force, tension.

   3. The centripetal force points towards the center of the circular path of motion.

B. The equation for the centripetal force is

$$\boxed{F_c = ma_c}$$

➤ F_c is the centripetal force, N

➤ m is the mass of the moving object, kg

➤ a is the centripetal acceleration, $\dfrac{m}{s^2}$

   1. The centripetal acceleration is a function of both the tangential velocity and the radius of the circular path:

$$\boxed{a_c = \frac{v^2}{r}}$$

➤ a_c is the centripetal acceleration, $\dfrac{m}{s^2}$

➤ v is the tangential velocity, $\dfrac{m}{s}$

➤ r is the radius of the circular path, m

Test Tip

The v in the centripetal acceleration equation is the same v in the equations shown above, giving $a_c = r\omega^2$ and $a_c = \dfrac{(4\pi^2 r)}{r^2}$.

$$a_c = r\omega^2 = \frac{v^2}{r} = \frac{(4\pi^2 r)}{r^2}$$

2. The centripetal acceleration describes the rate at which the direction of the tangential velocity is changing. Since velocity is a vector, the speed may remain the same, but since the direction of the velocity is always changing, the object is accelerating, as shown in Figure 6.2 below.

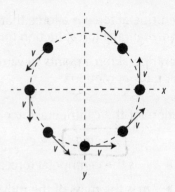

Figure 6.2

When an object moves in uniform circular motion, it is always accelerating, but the magnitude of the tangential velocity may remain constant.

III. FREE BODY DIAGRAMS

A. Free-Body Diagrams (FBD) are used to solve problems involving circular motion and centripetal force.

Common Situations for Centripetal Motion

Horizontal Motion:

Situation	FBD	Force Equations	The centripetal force is provided by
Car rounding a flat curve/child on a merry-go-round		$\Sigma F_x = f = ma_c$ $\Sigma F_y = n - mg = 0$	Static Friction
Car rounding a *banked* curve (no friction)		$\Sigma F_x = n \sin \theta = ma_c$ $\Sigma F_y = n \cos \theta - mg = 0$	The horizontal component of the Normal Force.
Conical pendulum		$\Sigma F_x = T \sin \theta = ma_c$ $\Sigma F_y = T \cos \theta - mg = 0$	The horizontal component of the Tension.

Vertical Motion:

Situation	FBD	Force Equations	The centripetal force is provided by
Mass on a string/ vertical roller coaster loop	TOP	$\Sigma F_x = 0$ $\Sigma F_y = -T - mg$ $= ma_c$	The sum of the Tension and Weight.
	BOTTOM	$\Sigma F_x = 0$ $\Sigma F_y = T - mg$ $= ma_c$	The difference of the Tension and Weight.

Situation	FBD	Force Equations	The centripetal force is provided by
Car on a hill/rider on Ferris wheel	TOP n *normal force* mg *weight*	$\Sigma F_x = 0$ $\Sigma F_y = n - mg$ $\quad = -ma_c$	The difference of the Weight and Normal Force.
	BOTTOM n *normal* mg *weight*	$\Sigma F_x = 0$ $\Sigma F_y = n - mg$ $\quad = ma_c$	The difference in the Normal Force and the Weight.

Test Tip

For the FBD shown above, the Tension and Normal Forces can be exchanged depending on the situation.

1. The minimum speed an object can have at the top of a loop, and still make it through the loop, is the *critical speed*.

2. At the top of the loop, the normal force or tension is momentarily equal to zero.

$$\Sigma F = -mg = -ma_c$$

$$mg = ma_c$$

$$g = a_c$$

$$g = \frac{v^2}{r}$$

$$\boxed{v_c = \sqrt{rg}}$$

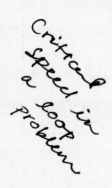

➤ v_c is the critical speed, $\frac{m}{s}$

➤ r is the radius of the circular path, m

➤ g is the acceleration due to gravity, $\frac{m}{s^2}$

3. Likewise, the maximum speed an object can have as it passes over the top of a hill and still stay in contact with the hill occurs when the normal force momentarily equals zero. Therefore, the maximum speed the object can have is the *critical speed*.

Test Tip

The critical speed should only be used in cases where the minimum or maximum speeds are required.

IV. PLANETARY MOTION

A. There is a gravitational force between all masses. It depends on the mass of the objects and the distance of separation between the two objects' center of mass.

$$N^{F_g} = \frac{Gm_1 m_2}{r^2} \quad \frac{\overline{\frac{Nm^2}{kg^2}} \cdot kg}{m}$$

> F_g is the gravitational force, N

> G is the gravitational constant, $6.67 \times 10^{-11} \dfrac{Nm^2}{kg^2}$

> m is the mass of each object, respectively, kg

> r is the distance of separation between the center of mass of each object, m

B. The gravitational force on each object is equal and opposite, which follows Newton's 3rd Law of Motion (N3L)

C. The gravitational force is <u>proportional to</u> $\left(\dfrac{1}{r^2} \right)$ which means it decreases exponentially as the distance between the two bodies increases.

$$F_g \propto \frac{1}{r^2}$$

D. In most physics problems, the orbit of a planet, moon or satellite may be assumed to be circular if $m_1 \gg m_2$

1. The gravitational force provides the centripetal force, as shown in Figure 6.3:

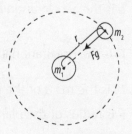

Figure 6.3

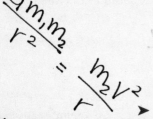

2. The orbital speed of the object, m_2, can be determined by setting the gravitational force equal to the centripetal force.

$$F_g = F_c$$

$$\frac{Gm_1 m_2}{r^2} = \frac{m_2 v^2}{r}$$

$$v = \sqrt{\frac{Gm_1}{r}}$$

➤ v is the orbital speed of m_2, $\dfrac{m}{s}$

➤ G is the gravitational constant, $6.67 \times 10^{-11} \dfrac{Nm^2}{kg^2}$

➤ r is the distance of separation between the center of mass of each body, m

E. An object located on the surface of a planet experiences a gravitational force, $F_g = \dfrac{Gm_1 m_2}{r^2}$ which is often referred to as the weight, mg, of the object.

$$F_g = \frac{Gm_1 m_2}{r^2} = m_2 g$$

Where m_2 is the mass located at the surface of the planet, m_1, then:

$$g = \frac{GM}{R^2}$$

➤ g is the acceleration due to gravity, $\dfrac{m}{s^2}$

➤ G is the gravitational constant, $6.67 \times 10^{-11} kg \dfrac{Nm^2}{s^2}$

➤ M is the mass of the planet, kg

➤ R is radius of the planet, m

Test Tip *The orbital speed is the tangential velocity. The equation for the orbital speed can be set equal to $r\omega$ or $\dfrac{2\pi r}{r}$.*

V. KEPLER'S LAWS OF PLANETARY MOTION

A. The orbital path of every planet is elliptical, with the Sun at one of the foci, as shown in Figure 6.4.

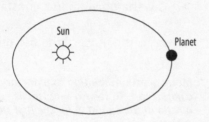

Sun
Planet

Figure 6.4

B. A line drawn from the planet to the Sun sweeps out an equal area in equal time on all points of the elliptical path, as shown in Figure 6.5.

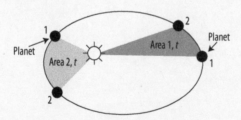

1
Planet
2
Planet
Area 1, *t*
Area 2, *t*
1
2

Figure 6.5

C. The time it takes for the mass to make one complete revolution, the *period*, is derived by setting the orbital speed equation to the speed of an object in circular motion.

$$v = \frac{2\pi r}{T} = \sqrt{\frac{Gm_1}{r}}$$

$$\frac{4\pi^2 r^2}{T^2} = \frac{Gm_1}{r}$$

$$T = \sqrt{\frac{4\pi^2 r^3}{Gm^2}}$$

➤ T is the period of the orbiting object, s

➤ r is the radius of the orbit, m

➤ G is the gravitational constant, $6.67 \times 10^{-11} \dfrac{Nm^2}{kg^2}$

➤ m_1 is the mass of the orbiting body, kg

Many questions relating to planetary motion will ask for comparison. To solve a problem like this, it is best to set up a ratio of the equation for the first situation to the second situation.

PART III

FLUID MECHANICS, KINETIC THEORY, AND THERMODYNAMICS

Fluid Mechanics

I. PRESSURE

A. A *fluid* is a liquid or gas. It can flow and fill the shape of a container.

B. *Pressure* is defined as the ratio of a force applied to a specific area.

$$P = \frac{F}{A}$$

➤ P is Pressure, measured in $\frac{N}{m^2} = Pa$ (Pascal)

➤ F is Force, measured in N

➤ A is Area, measured in m^2

C. *Hydrostatic pressure* refers to the pressure applied by the weight of a fluid. A column of fluid applies a pressure due to the weight of the fluid above it, as shown in Figure 7.1.

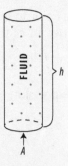

Figure 7.1

D. The pressure at the bottom of the column can be calculated by:

$$P = \frac{F}{A}$$

Where the *F* is the weight, *mg*

$$P = \frac{mg}{A}$$

E. Mass is not a commonly used measurement for fluids. Volume is most commonly used. The relationship between mass and volume is *density*.

$$\rho = \frac{m}{V}$$

➤ ρ is density, measured in $\frac{kg}{m^3}$

➤ *m* is mass, measured in *kg*

➤ *V* is volume, measured in *m³*

Therefore, the mass of the fluid can be described in terms of the density and the volume of the fluid.

$$m = \rho V$$

Substituting this for *m* in the pressure equation,

$$P = \frac{\rho V g}{A}$$

The volume of the column is the area of the base of the column multiplied by the height of the column.

$$V = Ah$$

Substituting this expression in for the volume:

$$P = \frac{\rho Ahg}{A}$$

Which simplifies to:

$$P = \rho g h$$

➤ P is Pressure, measured in $\dfrac{N}{m^2} = Pa$ (Pascal)

➤ ρ is density, measured in $\dfrac{kg}{m^3}$

➤ g is the acceleration of gravity, $\approx -10\dfrac{m}{s^2}$

➤ h is the height, or depth, of the column, measured in m

F. The pressure due to just the column of fluid is often referred to as the *gauge pressure*. Gauge pressure is the difference in the pressure applied to the top of the column of fluid, the atmospheric pressure, and the *absolute pressure*, which is the total pressure at the bottom of the column. Since atmospheric pressure is nearly constant and present, it is useful to describe the additional pressure applied because of the fluid.

$$P_{gauge} = P_A - P_o$$
$$P_{gauge} = \rho g h$$
$$P = P_o + \rho g h$$

➤ P_{gauge} is gauge pressure, P_a

➤ P is the absolute pressure, P_a

➤ P_o is the atmospheric pressure, $1.01 \times 10^5\ Pa$ at sea level.

G. The pressure at a given depth, h, is the same even if the shape of the container changes, as shown in figure 7.2.

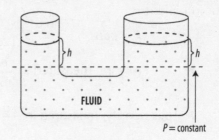

Figure 7.2

H. The force the pressure applied is perpendicular to the surface of the object the pressure is applied to, as shown in Figure 7.3.

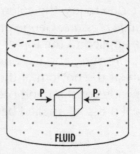

Figure 7.3

I. Pascal's principle states that for an enclosed fluid, an external pressure is transmitted undiminished and unchanged, throughout the fluid, as in Figure 7.4. This is the key to understanding hydraulics.

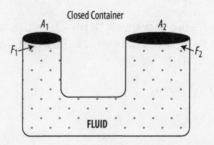

Figure 7.4

$$P_1 = P_2$$

$$\frac{F_1}{A_1} = \frac{F_2}{A_2}$$

1. This relationship shows that a small force applied to a small area will result in a larger force applied to a larger area. This allows for lifting objects that are much too heavy for humans.

II. BUOYANCY

A. When an object is placed in a fluid, the object will float or sink. In both cases, fluid is *displaced*. Archimedes' principle states: the weight of the fluid displaced is equal to the upward force exerted on the object by the fluid. This is called the *buoyant force*.

B. When an object floats, the upward force applied to the object, the buoyant force, is equal to the weight of the object.

$$F_{buoy} = mg$$

➤ F_{buoy} is the buoyant force, measured in *N*

➤ *m* is the mass, measured in *kg*

➤ *g* is the acceleration of gravity, $= 10\frac{m}{s^2}$

C. The buoyant force is the weight of the fluid displaced,

$$F_{buoy} = m_f g$$

Most fluids are not measured in terms of mass, but in terms of volume, so:

$$m = \rho V$$

Then the buoyant force is:

$$F_{buoy} = \rho_f V_f g$$

➤ F_{buoy} is the buoyant force, measured in N

➤ ρ_f is the density of the fluid displaced, measured in $\dfrac{kg}{m^3}$

➤ v_f is the volume of the fluid displaced, measured in m^3

➤ g is the acceleration of gravity, $10\dfrac{m}{s^2}$

D. When an object sinks, the buoyant force is less than the weight of the object. The volume of the fluid displaced is equal to the volume of the object. Since the forces are unbalanced, the object will accelerate downwards (until it reaches terminal velocity; drag friction cannot be ignored in this case).

Common Situations Involving Buoyant Force

Situation	FBD	Force Equations
Object floating, partially submerged	F_{buoy} ↑ □ ↓ mg	$\Sigma F_x = 0$ $\Sigma F_y = \rho_f V_f g - mg = 0$
Object floating, completely submerged (maximum weight of the object for floating)	F_{buoy} ↑ □ ↓ mg	$\Sigma F_x = 0$ $\Sigma F_y = \rho_f V_f g - mg = 0$ $V_{\text{fluid displaced}} = V_{\text{object}}$

Situation	FBD	Force Equations
Object sinking	F_{buoy} ↑ ▭ ↓ mg	$\Sigma F_x = 0$ $\Sigma F_y = \rho_f V_f g - mg = ma$ $V_{\text{fluid displaced}} = V_{\text{object}}$
Object suspended in a fluid, attached to a spring scale	F_{buoy} F_s ↑ ↑ ▭ ↓ mg	$\Sigma F_x = 0$ $\Sigma F_y = \rho_f V_f g + kx - mg = 0$ $V_{\text{fluid displaced}} = V_{\text{object}}$
Balloon floating in air	F_{buoy} ↑ ▭ ↓ mg	$\Sigma F_x = 0$ $\Sigma F_y = \rho_f V_f g - mg = 0$ *mg should include the mass of the balloon and the mass of the fluid *inside* the balloon.

III. FLUID FLOW CONTINUITY

A. Usually, liquids are considered *incompressible*, meaning that the density of the liquid remains nearly constant. Gases are easily compressed, i.e., air compressors for inflating tires and cans of compressed air for dusting electronics.

B. As a liquid flows from one container to another, the mass of liquid flowing from one section to another is equal,

$$m_1 = m_2$$

Therefore, in terms of density,

$$\rho V_1 = \rho V_2$$

The density doesn't change. The volume of liquid that passes through each section is equal,

$$V_1 = V_2$$

Figure 7.5 shows V_1 and V_2 as the liquid moves through the pipe. The volume can be calculated by:

$$V = Ax$$

$$A_1 x_1 = A_2 x_2$$

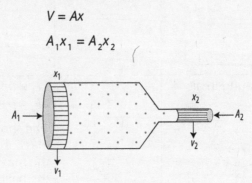

Figure 7.5

The liquid moves for the same amount of time, so both sides of the equation are divided by t:

$$\frac{A_1 x_1}{t} = \frac{A_2 x_2}{t}$$

$\frac{x}{t}$ is velocity, and substitution gives the *Continuity Equation*:

$$A_1 v_1 = A_2 v_2$$

➤ A is the cross-sectional area of the pipe, m^2

➤ v is the speed of the fluid in the pipe, $\frac{m}{s}$

C. Area times length is volume, $Ax = V$. The volume flow rate of the liquid in the pipe is constant.

$$\frac{V}{t} = Av$$

IV. BERNOULLI'S EQUATION

A. Bernoulli's equation is the conservation of energy applied to a moving fluid.

1. As a fluid moves from one chamber to another or from one high to another, as shown in Figure 7.6, work is done.

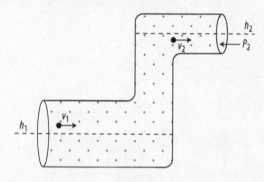

Figure 7.6

The general equation is:

$$P_1 + \frac{1}{2}\rho v_1^2 + \rho gh_1 = P_2 + \frac{1}{2}\rho v_2^2 + \rho gh_2$$

➤ P is the pressure, $\dfrac{N}{m^2}$

➤ ρ is the density of the fluid, $\dfrac{kg}{m^3}$

➤ v is the speed of the fluid, $\dfrac{m}{s}$

➤ g is the acceleration due to gravity, $\frac{m}{s^2}$

➤ h is the height of the fluid, m

2. Bernoulli's equation explains how an airplane wing (airfoil) experiences lift and how a fast-moving storm can lift the roof from a house.

3. A tank filled with a fluid, as shown in Figure 7.7, is open to the atmosphere at the top and has a rigid hole in the side. Because of the very small density of air, the pressure at the top is nearly equal to the pressure at the hole.

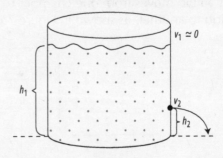

Figure 7.7

$$P_1 \approx P_2$$

The area of the opening at the top of the tank is much, much larger than the opening of the hole

$$A_1 >> A_2$$

According to the continuity equation:

$$A_1 v_1 = A_2 v_2$$

The speed of the fluid in the tank is much, much smaller than the speed of the fluid at the hole:

$$v_1 << v_2$$

So much smaller that $v_1 \approx 0$

Applying these conditions to Bernoulli's equation:

$$P_1 + \frac{1}{2}\rho(0) + \rho gh_1 = P_1 + \frac{1}{2}\rho v_2^2 + \rho gh_2$$

P_1 can be subtracted from both sides:

$$\rho gh_1 = \frac{1}{2}\rho v_2^2 + \rho gh_2$$

Divide by ρ on both sides:

$$gh_1 = \frac{1}{2}v_2^2 + gh_2$$

Solving for v_2:

$$v_2 = \sqrt{2g(h_1 - h_2)}$$

This equation is referred to as Torricelli's theorem.

Thermal Physics

I. MECHANICAL EQUIVALENT OF HEAT

A. James Prescott Joule, a British physicist, experimentally determined that thermal energy and mechanical energy are related.

B. *Heat* is the exchange of thermal energy between systems at different temperatures.

C. If a change in temperature occurs due to a mechanical process, the amount of thermal energy gained or lost is equal to the amount of mechanical energy lost or gained.

   1. The Law of Conservation of Energy states that energy cannot be created or destroyed, but rather only transferred from one system to another or transformed from one type to another.

   2. Mechanical energy is one form of energy while thermal energy is another. Friction can transform mechanical energy into thermal energy by heating the surfaces it contacts.

II. HEAT TRANSFER

A. *Conduction* is the transfer of thermal energy from one system to another through physical contact.

   1. *Conductors* are materials that allow thermal energy to flow easily.

2. *Insulators* are materials that do not allow thermal energy to flow easily.

3. The amount of thermal energy transferred or the amount of heat can be calculated:

$$H = kA\left(\frac{\Delta T}{L}\right)$$

➤ H is the rate for thermal energy transfer, $\frac{J}{s}$

➤ k is the thermal conductivity of a conductor. It is specific for each material, in $\frac{W}{mK}$

➤ A is the cross-sectional area of the conductor, m^2

➤ ΔT is the change in temperature, K

➤ L is the length of the conductor, m

B. Convection: as a fluid increases temperature, it expands. The body of fluid then rises, carrying the thermal energy with it. The surrounding lower temperature fluid falls, is heated, and then rises. Convection occurs due to uneven heating of fluids that in turn move the thermal energy.

C. Radiation: thermal energy transfers through electromagnetic waves. Electromagnetic waves are any waves in the electromagnetic spectrum: visible light, infrared light, and ultra-violet light.

1. All matter emits radiation.

2. The higher the temperature of the object, the higher the frequency of the radiation emitted.

III. THERMAL EXPANSION

A. When heated or cooled, most materials expand or contract, respectively.

B. The amount of expansion, for most materials, is a linear function.

$$\Delta L = \alpha L_o \Delta T$$

➤ ΔL is the change in length, *m*.

➤ α is the coefficient of expansion, $\dfrac{1}{K}$

➤ L_o is the initial length, *m*

➤ ΔT is the change in temperature, *K*.

C. Similar equations can be derived for both area and volume expansions.

IV. KINETIC THEORY

A. An ideal gas does not truly exist in nature, but dilute gases are very close approximations of ideal gas behavior. An ideal gas behaves according to the ideal gas law equation:

$$PV = nRT$$

➤ *P* is the pressure of the gas, *Pa*

➤ *V* is the volume of the gas, m^3

➤ *n* is the number of moles of gas, moles

➤ *R* is the universal gas constant. It is equivalent to $N_A k$, (Avogadro's number times Boltzman's constant) $= 8.31 \times \dfrac{J}{mol \cdot K}$

➤ *T* is the temperature, *K*.

1. The ideal gas law can also be written as:

$$PV = NkT$$

   ➤ N is the number of molecules

   ➤ k is Boltzman's constant $1.38 \times 10^{23} \dfrac{J}{K}$

2. For a closed container, where n is held constant, the ideal gas law can be written as a ratio:

$$\frac{P_1 V_1}{P_2 V_2} = \frac{nRT_1}{nRT_2}$$

   Since n is held constant and R is a constant, nR can be eliminated from the equation. This results in the *combined gas law equation*:

$$\frac{P_1 V_1}{T_1} = \frac{P_2 V_2}{T_2}$$

B. Due to the movement of the molecules of an ideal gas, each molecule has kinetic energy. The average kinetic energy of all molecules determines the temperature of the gas. Pressure is due to collisions between the molecules and the walls of the container.

1. The average kinetic energy of particles is directly related to the temperature of the gas and follows the following equation:

$$K_{AV} = \frac{3}{2} kT$$

   ➤ K_{AV} is the average kinetic energy of the particles, J

   ➤ k is Boltzman's constant $1.38 \times 10^{23} \dfrac{J}{K}$

   ➤ T is the temperature, measured in K

C. The average speed of a particle is:

$$\frac{1}{2}\mu v^2 = \frac{3}{2}kT$$

$$\mu v^2 = 3kT$$

$$v = \sqrt{\frac{3kT}{\mu}}$$

D. The mass of a molecule is the molar mass, *M*, divided by Avogadro's number, N_A.

$$\mu = \frac{M}{N_A}$$

$$v = \sqrt{\frac{3kT}{\frac{M}{N_A}}}$$

$$v = \sqrt{\frac{3kN_A T}{M}}$$

$$N_A k = R$$

$$v = \sqrt{\frac{3RT}{M}}$$

➤ *v* is the root-mean-square velocity, $\dfrac{m}{s}$

➤ *R* is the universal gas constant = $8.31\dfrac{J}{mol \cdot K}$

➤ *T* is the temperature, *K*

➤ *M* is the molar mass, $\dfrac{kg}{mol}$

E. The sum of all the individual energies of the molecules is the total internal energy of the gas, U.

$$U = NK_{AV}$$

$$U = \frac{3}{2}NkT$$

$$Nk = nR$$

$$U = \frac{3}{2}nRT$$

➤ U is the internal energy, J

➤ n is the number of moles of gas, moles

➤ R is the universal gas constant. $= 8.31\dfrac{J}{mol \cdot K}$

➤ T is the temperature, K

F. The ideal gas law is $PV = nRT$, which when compared to $U = \frac{3}{2}nRT$, gives:

$$PV = nRT = \frac{2}{3}U$$

V. LAWS OF THERMODYNAMICS

A. Zeroth Law: Thermal equilibrium is reached when two or more objects that are in thermal contact have the same temperature.

1. *Thermal contact* simply means that thermal energy can be exchanged between two objects. The objects do not have to be in physical contact.

B. First Law: The change in a gas's internal energy is dependent on the thermal energy added to or removed from the gas and the work done on the gas.

$$\Delta U = Q + W$$

➤ ΔU is the change in internal energy of a gas, J

➤ Q is the thermal energy added to (or removed from) the gas, J

➤ W is the work done on the gas, J

Most physics textbooks have this equation written as $\Delta U = Q - W$, where the work is described as done __by__ the gas. The equation shown above is written as given on the AP Exam Equation Sheet where the work is done __on__ the gas.

C. Second Law: Thermal energy naturally flows from the warmer object to the cooler object, never in the reverse direction.

D. Third Law: There is no temperature lower than absolute zero, and absolute zero is unattainable.

VI. PV DIAGRAMS AND THERMODYNAMIC PROCESSES

A. A PV diagram is a graph of pressure versus volume.

B. A line draw between two points on the graph can be described by a thermodynamic process, where thermal energy is transferred, work is done, or both.

C. A constant pressure (isobaric) process is one in which the pressure is held constant while the volume changes, as shown in Figure 8.1.

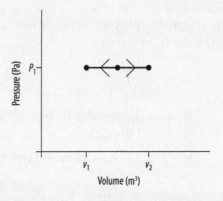

Figure 8.1

D. The volume can increase, shown by the right arrow, or decrease, shown by the left arrow.

1. When the volume increases, the gas expands, pushing on the environment.

2. A push is a force. Therefore, the gas is applying a force through a displacement, doing *work*.

   Work is force × distance

   $$W = Fd$$

   Pressure is force per area

   $$P = \frac{F}{A}$$

   Force is pressure × area

   $$W = PAd$$

   Area × distance is volume

   $$Ad = V$$

   Therefore, work done <u>by</u> the gas is pressure × change in volume

   $$W = P\Delta V$$

The work done <u>on</u> the gas is

$$W = -P\Delta V$$

➤ W is the work done by the environment on the gas, J

➤ P is the pressure of the gas, Pa

➤ ΔV is the change in volume of the gas, measured in m^3

Test Tip

When a gas expands, $\Delta V > 0$, the gas does positive work, but the work done on the gas is negative. When a gas contracts, $\Delta V < 0$, negative work is being done by the gas, and the environment applies a force doing positive work.

3. For a PV diagram, the area under the curve is the work done on or by the gas, as shown in Figure 8.2.

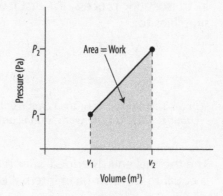

Figure 8.2

Test Tip

In an isobaric expansion (drawn left to right on a PV diagram), the temperature of the gas increases along with its internal energy.

E. A constant volume (or isochoric, isovolumetric or isometric) process is one in which the volume is held constant and the pressure changes, as shown in Figure 8.3.

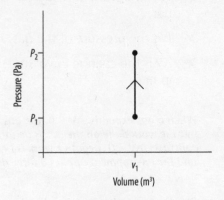

Figure 8.3

i. In an isochoric process, the first law of thermodynamics simplifies to:

$$\Delta U = Q$$

In an isochoric process, the volume of the gas does not change. Therefore, no work is done on or by the gas.

ii. The thermal energy added to or removed from the gas is equal to the change in internal energy of the gas.

In an isochoric pressurization (drawn upwards on a PV diagram), the temperature of the gas increases as well as its internal energy.

F. An isothermal process is one in which the temperature does not change; thus, *nRT* in the ideal gas law equation is constant, meaning the *PV* cannot change. An *isotherm* has the shape of a hyperbola, as shown in Figure 8.4.

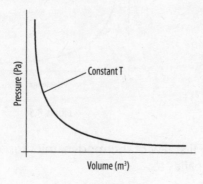

Figure 8.4

1. In an isothermal process, the first law of thermodynamics simplifies to:

$$Q = -W$$

2. The thermal energy added to the gas is equal to the negative work done on the gas (the gas does positive work on the environment as the gas expands).

Test Tip

In an isothermal process, the gas temperature does not change; therefore, the internal energy, U, does not change (ΔU=0)

G. An adiabatic process is one in which no thermal energy is exchanged with the gas, *Q* = 0. An *adiabat* is similar in shape to an isotherm, but must descend more steeply than a hyperbola, as shown in Figure 8.5.

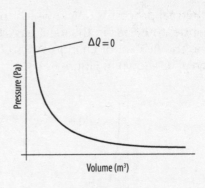

Figure 8.5

1. The first law of thermodynamics for an adiabatic process simplifies to:

$$\Delta U = W$$

2. The change in internal energy is equal to the work done on the gas.

In an adiabatic expansion, the volume increases as both the pressure and temperature decrease. Since the temperature decreases, so does the internal energy.

VII. HEAT ENGINES AND EFFICIENCY

A. In general, efficiency is the ratio of work done by a system to the energy put into the system.

$$e = \frac{W}{Q_H}$$

➤ e is the efficiency, no units

➤ W is the work done by a system, J

➤ Q_n is the thermal energy added to the system, J

B. A *heat* engine is a device that transforms thermal energy into work, such as a steam engine.

1. Water is heated to steam; the steam pushes a piston and cools off; the cool water is pumped back to the boiler and the process starts again.

2. The maximum theoretical efficiency of a heat engine depends on the temperatures of the two reservoirs.

   i. The work done is the difference in the thermal energy added to the system in the hot reservoir, Q_H, and the thermal energy left in the cold reservoir, Q_C, after the work is done.

   $$W = Q_H - Q_C$$

   ii. Efficiency is the work done divided by the thermal energy supplied,

   $$e = \frac{W}{Q_H} = \frac{(Q_H - Q_C)}{Q_H} = 1 - \frac{Q_C}{Q_H}$$

   ➤ *e* is the efficiency

   ➤ *W* is the work done, J

   ➤ Q_H is the thermal energy transferred from the hot reservoir, J

   ➤ Q_C is the thermal energy transferred to the cold reservoir, J

C. A Carnot engine is a theoretical heat engine that operates at maximum efficiency between two temperatures, and the processes are completely reversible.

1. The efficiency of a Carnot engine depends on the temperature, T_H, of the environment from which the thermal energy is transferred to the engine, Q_H and the temperature, T_C, of the environment to which the thermal energy is transferred from the engine, Q_C.

   $$\frac{Q_H}{Q_C} = \frac{T_H}{T_C}$$

This proportionality can be substituted into the efficiency equation:

$$e = 1 - \frac{T_C}{T_H}$$

➤ e is the efficiency

➤ T_C is the cold reservoir temperature, K

➤ T_H is the hot reservoir temperature, K

2. The Carnot engine cycle consists of four processes, as shown in Figure 8.6, two isothermal and two adiabatic processes.

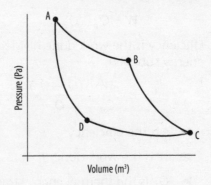

Figure 8.6

➤ Process A to B = isothermal ($\Delta U = 0$)

➤ Process B to C = adiabatic ($Q = 0$)

➤ Process C to D = isothermal ($\Delta U = 0$)

➤ Process D to A = adiabatic ($Q = 0$)

VIII. Cyclic Processes

A. The work done by a gas during a cyclic process is the area enclosed by the function on the graph.

B. A "clock-wise" process is one in which net positive work is done by the gas, as shown in Figure 8.7(a).

C. A "counter-clockwise" process is one in which net negative work is done by the gas, as shown in Figure 8.7(b).

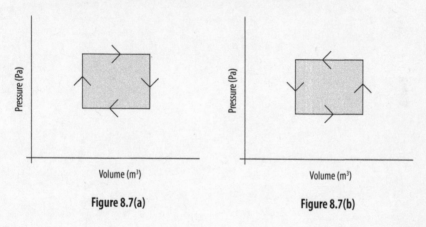

Figure 8.7(a)   Figure 8.7(b)

PART IV
ELECTRICITY AND MAGNETISM

Static Electricity

I. COULOMB'S LAW—ELECTRIC FORCE

A. Protons, neutrons and electrons make up all objects. Protons are positively charged and electrons are negatively charged. Both particles have the same amount of charge, but opposite signs. The magnitude of the charge on an electron is:

$$e = 1.602 \times 10^{19} \text{ C}$$

    1. Placing a negative sign or a positive sign in front of this value denotes that the particle is an electron or proton, respectively.

B. The unit of charge, C, is named for Charles Coulomb.

C. The symbol used for charge is q (or Q for large quantities of charge).

D. "Opposite" charges attract, that is, they apply a mutual attractive force.

    1. According to Newton's 3rd Law, this force must be equal and opposite.

    2. Conversely, "like" charges repel. Again the forces on each must be equal and opposite.

E. Figure 9.1(a) shows the forces between two "opposite" charges. Charge, q_1, applies an attractive force, F_2 on q_2 to the left, while q_2 applies an attractive force, F_1, on q_1. Figure 9.1(b) shows the forces between two "like" charges. In both cases, the magnitudes of the forces are equal.

$F_1 = -F_2$

$-F_3 = F_4$

Figure 9.1(a)   **Figure 9.1(b)**

Use the force relationship to define the direction of the forces between charges, and take the absolute value of the charges to find the magnitude of the force between the two charges.

F. The force between charges can be calculated using Coulomb's Law equation.

$$F = \frac{1}{4\pi\varepsilon_o} \frac{|q_1||q_2|}{r^2}$$

➤ F is the electric force between two charges, N

➤ $\frac{1}{4\pi\varepsilon_o}$ is proportionally constant, often referred to as

$$k = 9.0 \times 10^9 \frac{Nm^2}{C^2}$$

Coulomb's Law equation is provided on the AP Physics B exam equation sheet as shown here; however, most textbooks use the k variation, $F = k\dfrac{|q_1||q_2|}{r^2}$

➤ q_1 and q_2 are the charges in absolute value, C

➤ r is the distance between the two charges, m

Notice the similarities between the gravitational force between two masses, $F_g = \dfrac{Gm_1m_2}{r^2}$ and the electric force between two charges $F = k\dfrac{|q_1||q_2|}{r^2}$. Both are called "inverse-square-laws."

G. Since force is a vector, the force between two charges must be treated as a vector. When more than one charge applies a force to a *q*, the forces of each charge are summed up using *superposition*. An example of superposition is shown in Figure 9.2.

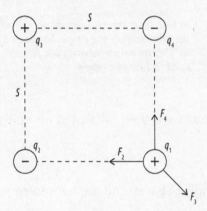

Figure 9.2

1. In the figure shown above, F_2 is the attractive force applied to $+q_1$ due to $-q_2$; F_3 is the repulsive force applied to $+q_1$ due to $+q_3$; F_4 is the attractive force applied to $+q_1$ due to q_4. The magnitude of each of the forces can be calculated using Coulomb's Law equation.

H. To solve for the net force acting on q_1, as shown in Figure 9.2, it is useful to create a Free-Body Diagram, as shown in Figure 9.3.

FBD

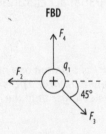

Figure 9.3

Summing the forces in the x and y directions will give the net x and y components of the force.

$$F_x = -F_2 + F_3 \cos 45$$

$$F_y = F_4 - F_3 \sin 45$$

In this case, the charges are arranged at the corners of a square, making the angle between F_3 and the x axis 45°. Not all charge arrangements are squares, and geometry must be used to find the angle.

The resultant is then calculated using Pythagorean's Theorem:

$$F_R = \sqrt{F_x^2 + F_y^2}$$

The angle between the resultant force and the x axis is:

$$\theta = \tan^{-1}\left(\frac{F_y}{F_x}\right)$$

Often free-response questions will require students to provide answers in terms of given quantities and fundamental constants. The ratios of common angles are provided on the Table of Information sheet. Be familiar with how to answer questions in pure variable form.

I. Just as with any force, the electric force can be equated to *ma*, solving for the initial acceleration of the particle at the instant it is released.

The mass of a proton and an electron are provided on the Table of Information sheet. The mass of a proton is approximately 1000 times larger than the mass of an electron.

II. **ELECTRIC FIELD**

A. The electric force is a conservative force. The electric force is similar in nature to the gravitational force. An electric force is applied to a charge, *q*, while in an *electric field, E.*

$$F = |q|E$$

➤ *F* is the electric force, *N*

➤ *q* is the charge in the electric field, *C*

➤ *E* is the electric field, $\dfrac{N}{C}$

B. Comparing this equation to Coulomb's Law equation,

$$E = \frac{1}{4\pi\varepsilon_o} \frac{|Q|}{r^2}$$

This is the electric field created by a point charge, *Q*.

C. The electric field is a vector quantity that points in the direction that a *positive test charge* would be forced if placed near the source charge, as shown in Figure 9.4.

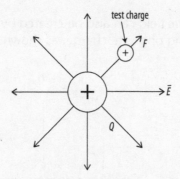

Figure 9.4

The *test charge, q,* would be repelled by the source charge, *+Q,* giving an electric field pointing *away* from the positive source charge.

D. Electric field lines are always perpendicular to the surface of the source. The number of field lines drawn is proportional to the size of the source charge.

E. Since the direction of the electric field is defined by the direction that a positive test charge would move, electric field lines are always drawn from positive charge to negative charge, as shown in Figure 9.5.

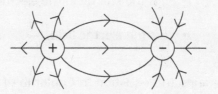

Figure 9.5

 *Since a positive charge is used to define the direction of the electric field, a positive charge placed in the electric field would be force in the direction of the electric field. A negative charge behaves oppositely; a negative charge placed in an electric field would be forced against the electric field.*

F. An electric field can also be created by two parallel plates containing opposite charge, as shown in Figure 9.6.

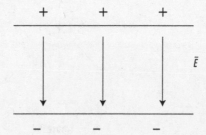

Figure 9.6

G. The electric field created by the parallel plates is a *uniform* electric field; its magnitude is the same at all points between the two plates. Two parallel plates form a *capacitor*.

Electric fields created by a point charge obey the equation,

$E = \dfrac{k|Q|}{r^2}$; however, electric fields created by parallel plates are uniform, *and do not depend on the distance from the charge,* r. *Thus the only equation that can be used for uniform electric*

fields is $E = \dfrac{F}{|q|}$.

H. The resultant electric field can be calculated using superposition. Adding all the individual electric field contributions at a point results in the net electric field at that point.

I. The electric field is a vector, and must be added using vector addition.

J. The electric field on a line midway between two like charges is zero.

K. The electric field between two "opposite" charges can never be zero. The electric field is zero at a point *outside* the charge of smaller magnitude.

The electric force on a charge in a uniform *electric field is* F = | q| E.

L. The net electric field at a point due to several charges is shown in Figure 9.7.

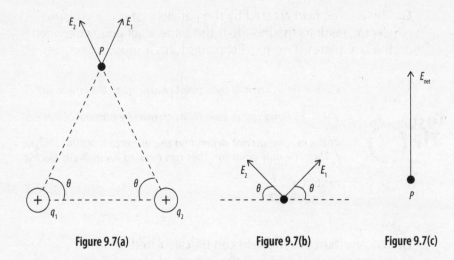

Figure 9.7(a) Figure 9.7(b) Figure 9.7(c)

q_1 and q_2 lie on the bottom corners of a triangle. Point P is located at the top of the triangle. Each positive charge applies an electric field at point P in the direction indicated in Figure 9.7(a). In this case, each electric field is at an angle to the x axis, as shown in Figure 9.7(b). The net electric field is in the positive y direction, as shown in Figure 9.7(c). The magnitude of each electric field can be solved for using $E = \dfrac{k|Q|}{r^2}$. Vector addition is used to determine the resulting electric field.

Know how to draw the electric field lines around a charge and at a point from a charge or multiple charges. If multiple charges, be able to estimate the net electric field at a point.

III. INSULATORS AND CONDUCTORS

A. An *insulator* is a material that does not allow charge to move easily. Wood, plastic, and rubber are insulators.

B. A *conductor* is a material that allows charge to move easily. Examples include metals and salt water.

C. When excess charge is placed on an insulator, the charge is "stuck" and cannot move. The excess charge creates an electric field.

D. When excess charge is placed on a conductor, the charge moves to the outermost area, the surface of the conductor.

E. The electric field inside a conductor in electrostatic equilibrium is zero, no matter the charge on the conductor. This is referred to as *electric field shielding,* shown in Figure 9.8.

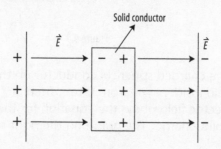

Figure 9.8

1. When the conductor is placed in the electric field, the electrons are attracted to the left parallel plate. This sets up an *induced charge* on the conductor. The net charge on the conductor is zero. The electric field set up by two parallel plates, ends on the left surface of the solid conductor inserted between the two plates, and begins again on the right side of the conductor. There is no electric field inside the conductor.

When a negatively charged object is brought near a second object that is grounded, the negatively charged object will force electrons out of the second object to the ground, leaving a net positive charge on the second object. Alternately, if the object is positively charged, it will draw electrons from the ground, leaving the second object negatively charged.

F. The magnitude of the electric field outside a conducting sphere is equal in magnitude to the electric field of an equal point charge at the same distance from the center of the sphere. A graph of the magnitude of the electric field of a conducting sphere vs. the distance from the center is shown in Figure 9.9.

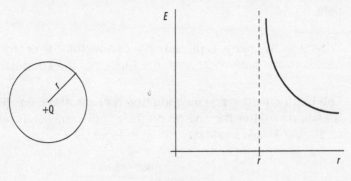

Figure 9.9

1. The charged spherical conductor on the left has zero electric field inside, $E = 0$ from 0 to r, then at r the function for the electric field obeys the equation for the electric field of a point charge. The graph on the right shows the function.

G. When an uncharged, neutral, conductor is placed near a charge, a surface charge is induced on the conductor. In Figure 9.10(a), a charge $+Q$ is surrounded by a spherical shell conductor with no net charge. Figure 9.10(b) shows negative charge induced on the inner surface of the shell, leaving a positive charge on the surface of the conductor. Since the inner $+Q$ attracts an equal $-Q$ on the inner surface a $+Q$ is left on the surface of the conductor.

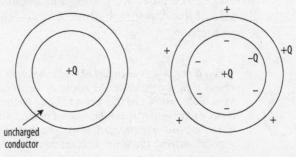

Figure 9.10(a)   **Figure 9.10(b)**

1. The net charge on the "system" shown in Figure 9.10b is +Q. The uncharged conductor does not contribute to the net charge. A graph of the electric field vs. radial distance is shown in Figure 9.11.

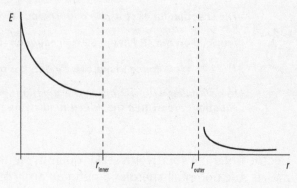

Figure 9.11

IV. ELECTRIC POTENTIAL ENERGY

A. When charges are separated by a distance, there is a force between them. If released, the force will cause the charges to move, thus giving the charges kinetic energy. The kinetic energy of the charges come from the stored *potential* energy in the arrangement of the charges.

B. Electric potential energy can be calculated using:

$$U = \frac{1}{4\pi\varepsilon_o} \frac{q_1 q_2}{r}$$

➤ U is the electric potential energy, J

➤ $\frac{1}{4\pi\varepsilon_o}$ is a proportionally constant, often referred to as $k = 9.0 \times 10^9 \frac{Nm^2}{C^2}$

➤ q_1 and q_2 are the charges, C

➤ r is the distance between the two charges, m

C. Electric potential energy is *not* an absolute value. The potential energy between two like charges is positive, while the potential energy between two opposite charges is negative.

The equation for electric potential energy $\left(U = \dfrac{1}{4\pi\varepsilon_o}\dfrac{q_1 q_2}{r} \right)$ is provided on the AP Physics B exam equation sheet; however, $U = \dfrac{kq_1 q_2}{r}$ is found in most textbooks. It is a good idea to be familiar with what is on the equation sheet. How the equations are written should not hinder you.

D. Electric potential energy is a scalar quantity, so the sum of all the electric potential energies among an array of charges gives the net electric potential energy of the system.

$$U_{net} = U_1 + U_2 + U_3 \ldots$$

1. The net electric potential energy of a system of four charges located at the corners of a triangle, as shown in Figure 9.12, is equal to the sum of the individual electric potential energies of each pair.

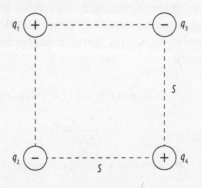

Figure 9.12

For example:

$$U_{net} = \frac{kq_1 q_2}{s} + \frac{kq_1 q_3}{s} + \frac{kq_1 q_4}{s\sqrt{2}} + \frac{kq_3 q_4}{s} + \frac{kq_3 q_2}{s\sqrt{2}} + \frac{kq_4 q_2}{s}$$

E. The electric force is a conservative force, and the work done by a conservative force is

$$W_o = -\Delta U$$

F. The work done by the electric force is opposite to the change in electric potential energy. When a positive charge moves in the same direction as the electric field, the work done by the field is positive and the charge loses electric potential energy.

V. ELECTRIC POTENTIAL

A. *Electric potential* is the amount of energy that is available per charge at any given location from a source charge, Q.

B. The electric potential around a point charge is equal at all points r from the charge and can be calculated using

$$V = \frac{1}{4\pi\varepsilon_o} \sum_i \frac{q_i}{r_i}$$

➤ V is the electric potential, $\frac{J}{C}$

➤ $\frac{1}{4\pi\varepsilon_o}$ is a proportionally constant, often referred to as

$$k = 9.0 \times 10^9 \frac{Nm^2}{C^2}$$

➤ q_i is the ith charge, C

➤ r_i is the distance from the ith charge to the point in question, m

The equation $V = \frac{1}{4\pi\varepsilon_o} \sum_i \frac{q_i}{r_i}$ is given on the AP Physics B exam equation sheet. However, most textbooks provide $V = \frac{kQ}{r}$.

C. Electric potential is also a scalar, so the sum of the electric potentials at a point is the sum of the individual electric potentials due to each charge.

D. By definition, *electric potential* is the electric potential energy per charge.

$$V = \frac{U}{q}$$

Therefore,

$$U = qV$$

➤ q is the charge placed at the point, C

➤ V is the electric potential at the point, $\frac{J}{C}$

> A common application of the electric potential energy is in the case where a charge is accelerated through a potential difference. The electric potential energy is converted to kinetic energy, $qV = \frac{1}{2}mv^2$.

E. The electric potential around a point charge can be described by equipotential surfaces, as shown in Figure 9.13.

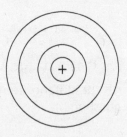

Figure 9.13

1. Equipotential lines are drawn as concentric circles around a point charge, denoting that the potential at each position is the same. In general, equipotential lines are drawn connecting points of equal electric potential.

F. It is assumed for this course that the electric field between two plates of opposite charge is uniform. The electric potential and the electric field is related by

$$V = Ed$$

➤ *V* is the electric potential, $\frac{J}{C}$

➤ *E* is the *uniform* electric field, $\frac{N}{C}$

➤ *d* is the distance between the two points containing the *E, m*

G. As defined by a positive test charge, electric field lines point away from a positive source charge. The electric potential *decreases* as the distance from the source charge increases. Electric field lines run from high electric potential to low electric potential.

H. The electric force is conservative. The work done by the electric field is

$$W_E = -\Delta U = -q\Delta V$$

The work done by any conservative force is equal to the negative change in potential energy.

Test Tip

When positive charges move in the same direction as the electric field, they move from high electric potential to low electric potential and lose potential energy. When negative charges move against the electric field, they move from low electric potential to high electric potential, but they still lose potential energy.

I. The electric field inside a conductor in electrostatic equilibrium is zero, the electric potential at the surface of the conductor must be constant. There is no difference in electric potential between any two points on the surface.

Current Electricity

CURRENT, RESISTANCE, AND VOLTAGE

A. *Current* is defined as the amount of charge moving past a specific point in a conductor per time.

$$I = \frac{Q}{t}$$

➤ I is the current, $\frac{C}{s} = A$ (Amperes)

➤ Q is the amount of charge, C

➤ t is the time, s

B. In order for current to flow, charges need a conductor. A *conductor* is a material that allows the charge to move freely.

  1. Every conductor contains atoms, which contain protons and neutrons in the nucleus and electrons in the energy levels surrounding the nucleus.

  2. In metallic conductors, electrons are the charge carriers and are free to move once a potential difference, V, is applied to the conductor.

C. The *conventional current* is described by the direction that *positive* charges would move.

D. As the charges move through the conductor, collisions with subatomic particles occur. This inherent property is the *resistance*.

E. Resistance of a material is analogous to the "friction" experienced by a particle moving on a rough surface.

F. The *resistivity* of a material is specific to its atomic makeup.

G. The resistance of a conductor can be calculated by using:

$$R = \frac{\rho l}{A}$$

➤ *R* is the resistance of the conductor, Ω, Ohm

➤ ρ is the resistivity of the material, $\frac{\Omega}{m}$

➤ *l* is the length of the conductor, *m*

➤ *A* is the cross-sectional area of the conductor, m^2

1. Figure 10.1 shows each of the dimensions described above.

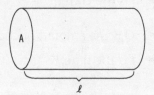

Figure 10.1

H. A potential difference, *V*, is needed to cause charges to move through a conductor. A potential difference indicates that an electric field exists, the electric field applies a force to the free charges, thus creating a current.

1. In circuits, potential difference is usually referred to as *voltage* and the unit, $\frac{J}{C}$, is referred to as the *volt, V*.

Test Tip

A potential difference is analogous to a height difference needed to get a ball to roll down a ramp.

I. Putting V, R, and I together, Georg Ohm found that as the voltage applied to a conductor increases, the current through the conductor also increases. This relationship leads to Ohm's Law:

$$V = IR$$

➤ *V* is the voltage applied to the conductor, *V*

➤ *I* is the current through the conductor, *A*

➤ *R* is the resistance of the conductor, Ω

Test Tip

The resistance of a material is the slope of a voltage vs. current graph or the inverse of the slope of a current vs. voltage graph.

II. POWER

A. *Power* is defined mechanically as work per time, which is

$$\frac{J}{s} = \text{watt}$$

B. In electricity, *J/s = watt,* can be derived from the units of voltage and current.

$$P = IV$$

➤ *P* is the power, $\frac{J}{s}$ = watts *(W)*

➤ *I* is the current, *A*

➤ *V* is the voltage, *J/C = volt (V)*

C. Substituting Ohm's Law into the power equation gives:

$$P = IV = I^2R = \frac{V^2}{R}$$

D. Power is the rate at which energy is used or developed.

$$P = \frac{E}{t}$$

Therefore,

$$E = Pt$$

A substitution for P is

$$E = IVt$$

➤ E is energy, J

➤ I is the current, A

➤ V is the voltage, $\frac{J}{C} = V$

➤ t is the time, s

Always check the units of given quantities. If the power is a quantity given, it may be written as "the rate at which energy is used in the circuit is 10 $\frac{J}{C}$." Here the definition of power was used rather than the word power.

III. CIRCUITS AND CIRCUIT DIAGRAMS

A. A circuit is a closed path and electric current can flow.

B. An open circuit is *not* closed and electric current cannot flow.

C. A short circuit is a path of essentially zero resistance—the "shortest" path back to the battery.

D. Circuit diagrams are schematics designed to show the components of the circuit and the direction of the conventional current. The table below shows common components and their corresponding symbol:

Component	Symbol
Wire	————
Battery	—+‖—‖—
Resistor	—⋀⋀⋀—
Capacitor	—‖—‖—
Switch	•—•╱—•

E. Resistors are drawn to represent the resistance of the load on the circuit.

    1. For most diagrams, the wires are considered to have zero resistance.

F. Resistors can be wired in *series*.

    1. Figure 10.2 shows a diagram of three resistors in series.

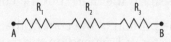

Figure 10.2

2. As shown, resistors wired in series are connected one after another, from *A* to *B*.

   i. When connected to a battery, current will flow through the resistors.

   ii. Each resistor will get the same current, but the voltage across each will depend on the resistance of each, according to Ohm's Law, $V = IR$.

   iii. The larger resistors will receive the most voltage, and the most power will be dissipated through the largest resistor, according to $P = IV$.

G. The sum of the resistance of resistors in series, the equivalent resistance, is:

$$R_S = R_1 + R_2 + R_3 + \dots$$

H. Resistors can be wired in parallel.

1. Figure 10.3 shows a diagram of three resistors in parallel.

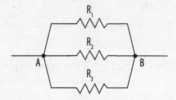

Figure 10.3

2. As shown, resistors wired in parallel are connected at junctions, *A* and *B*, as shown.

   i. When connected to a battery, the voltage across each resistor is the same, but the current splits at the junction.

   ii. The portion of the current that travels through each resistor will depend on the resistance of each, according to Ohm's Law, $V = IR$.

   iii. The smaller resistor will get the most current, and the most power will be dissipated through the smallest resistor, according to $P = IV$.

Test Tip

Current always "chooses" the path of least resistance.

I. The sum of the resistance of resistors in parallel, the equivalent resistance, is:

$$\frac{1}{R_p} = \frac{1}{R_1} + \frac{1}{R_2} + \frac{1}{R_3} \dots$$

Test Tip

The equivalent resistance for identical resistors, R, in parallel is $\frac{R}{2}$.

J. The arrangement of resistors, series or parallel, affects the current through the circuit and the voltage across each resistor. The table below summarizes the relationships:

	Series	Parallel
Voltage across resistor (V_T)	$V_T = V_1 + V_2 + V_3 + \dots$	$V_T = V_1 = V_2 = V_3 = \dots$
Current through branch (I_T)	$I_T = I_1 = I_2 = I_3 = \dots$	$I_T = I_1 + I_2 + I_3 + \dots$

K. The total resistance of circuits containing resistors in series and parallel should be calculated by breaking the circuit in to series and parallel portions.

1. The total resistance can be used to find the current through the battery.

2. Start at the positive side of the battery and trace the current as it flows through the circuit; this helps define which resistors are in series and which resistors are in parallel.

3. An example is shown in Figure 10.4.

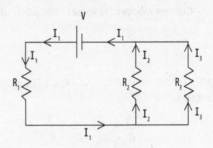

Figure 10.4

i. Starting at the positive side of the battery, V, the conventional current, I_1, flows down through R_1, and breaks into I_2 and I_3 (this indicates that R_1 and R_2 are in parallel). After I_2 and I_3 pass through R_2 and R_3, respectively, they combine to form I_1 again. I_1 passes through the battery, which indicates that the battery is wired in series with R_1.

Test Tip

There are a variety of ways to draw circuits. Be familiar with different variations of circuit diagram design.

L. Light bulbs are often drawn in a circuit.

1. If the resistance is the same for each, light bulbs with the most current are the brightest.

2. If a light bulb is removed from a series of light bulbs, all the lights will go out.

3. If a light bulb is removed from a parallel circuit of light bulbs, only the one removed will go out. The others will stay lit and will burn brighter.

IV. TERMINAL VOLTAGE AND KIRCHHOFF'S LAWS

A. All batteries have internal resistance, usually denoted by *r*. The *terminal voltage* of a battery is the ideal voltage of the battery minus the voltage drop across the internal resistance in a closed circuit.

1. The ideal voltage of the battery is the *emf, ε*. Emf stands for *electromotive force*.

2. The electromotive force is not a real force as once believed, but the term is still used to describe the voltage of a battery.

3. Figure 10.5 shows an example of a battery drawn with its internal resistance.

A ε r   B   I

Figure 10.5

4. The terminal voltage, V_{AB}, can be calculated by adding the voltage across each component. In this case, the conventional current runs from *A* to *B*.

$$V_{AB} = \varepsilon - Ir$$

Test Tip

If the current through the circuit flows "backward" through a battery, there is a voltage drop, or loss. In the case of the terminal voltage, $V_{AB} = -\varepsilon - Ir$.

B. Kirchhoff's Laws are useful in simple circuits and in circuits containing multiple batteries on different branches.

C. The *junction rule*, also referred to as the point rule, states that all the current entering a junction must leave that junction.

$$\Sigma I = 0$$

1. An example of a junction is shown in Figure 10.6.

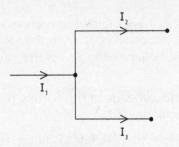

Figure 10.6

2. For the example shown above, a junction rule equation can be written as:

$$I_1 = I_2 + I_3$$

D. The junction rule represents the conservation of charge.

E. The *loop rule* states that the sum of all the potential differences around a closed loop is zero.

$$\Sigma V = 0$$

1. An example of a loop is shown in Figure 10.7.

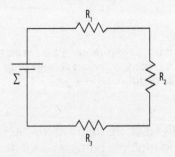

Figure 10.7

2. For the example shown above, a loop rule equation can be written as:

$$\Sigma V = \varepsilon - IR_1 - IR_2 - IR_3 = 0$$

3. When following the current through the loop, there is a gain in voltage as the current leaves the positive side of the battery and there is a loss of voltage as the current passes through a resistor.

V. CAPACITORS

A. Capacitors are electric components that store charge, thus storing energy. The most common type of capacitor is a parallel plate capacitor, as shown in Figure 10.8.

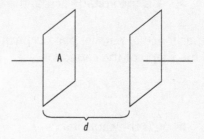

Figure 10.8

B. The capacity of charge that can be held is referred to as the *capacitance* and is a function of the geometrical shape of the capacitor plates.

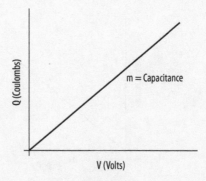

Figure 10.9

C. A graph of the voltage vs. the charge is shown in Figure 10.9. The slope of the line is the capacitance.

$$C = \frac{\Delta Q}{\Delta V}$$

Commonly written as the amount of charge on each plate:

$$Q = CV$$

➤ Q is the charge on each plate, C

➤ C is the capacitance of the capacitor, F

➤ V is the voltage across the capacitor, V

D. The capacitance of parallel plate capacitor depends on the geometric shape of the capacitor.

$$C = \frac{\varepsilon_o A}{d}$$

➤ C is the capacitance, F

➤ ε_o is the permittivity of free space, $8.85 \times 10^{-12} \frac{F}{m}$

➤ A is the surface area of one of the plates, m^2

➤ d is the distance of separation between the two plates, m

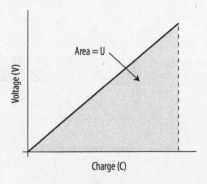

Figure 10.10

E. The area under the curve on a voltage vs. charge graph represents the energy stored in the capacitor, as shown in Figure 10.10. The calculation of the stored energy is:

$$U = \frac{1}{2}QV$$

And using the equation $Q = CV$

$$U = \frac{1}{2}CV^2 = \frac{1}{2}\frac{Q^2}{C}$$

F. Capacitors can be combined in series and parallel circuits.

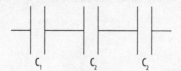

Figure 10.11

1. Series capacitors, as shown in Figure 10.11, are added together by:

$$\frac{1}{C} = \frac{1}{C_1} + \frac{1}{C_2} + \frac{1}{C_3}\ldots$$

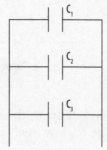

Figure 10.12

2. Parallel capacitors, as shown in Figure 10.12, are added by:

$$C = C_1 + C_2 + C_3 + ...$$

	Series	Parallel
Voltage across capacitor (V_T)	$V_T = V_1 + V_2 + V_3 + ...$	$V_T = V_1 = V_2 = V_3 = ...$
Charge on capacitor (Q_T)	$Q_T = Q_1 = Q_2 = Q_3 = ...$	$Q_T = Q_1 + Q_2 + Q_3 + ...$

Test Tip *Unlike resistors, voltage is inversely related to the capacitance of the capacitor because of Q = CV.*

VI. RC CIRCUITS

A. An *RC circuit* is one that contains resistor(s) and capacitor(s), as shown in Figure 10.13.

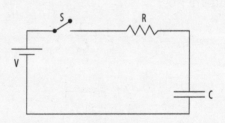

Figure 10.13

B. When the switch is flipped, the capacitor charges. The capacitor allows for charge to flow freely into it. The capacitor behaves as a wire.

C. In Figure 10.14, the initial current through the resistor would be $\frac{V}{R}$; the voltage across the capacitor would be zero; and the voltage across the resistor would be *V*.

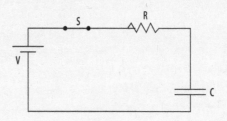

Figure 10.14

D. If the switch in Figure 10.14 has been closed for a very long time, the capacitor is full. The current in the circuit ceases. This means the voltage across *R* is now zero and the voltage across the capacitor is *V*.

For your AP Physics B exam be sure you're comfortable with the different variations of simple RC circuit arrangements.

Magnetism

I. THE MAGNETIC FORCE ON A MOVING CHARGE

A. Experimentally it was determined that a force is applied to a charged particle when moving through a magnetic field with a non-parallel velocity. The force was determined to be perpendicular to the plane of the velocity and magnetic field.

   1. Magnetic field is measured in Tesla.

   2. The magnitude of the force on a charge moving in a magnetic field is:

$$F_B = qvB \sin \theta$$

   ➤ F_B is the magnitude of the magnetic force, N

   ➤ q is the magnitude of the charge, C

   ➤ v is the magnitude of the velocity, m/s

   ➤ B is the magnitude of the magnetic field, T

   ➤ θ is the angle between the velocity and the magnetic field vectors, degrees

The magnetic force, being perpendicular to the plane of the velocity vector and magnetic field vector, results in vectors in three-dimensional space. Commonly, the plane of the page is used as a reference in such problems. The horizontal dimension of the page is the x-axis, the vertical dimension of the page is the y-axis and "in or out" of the page is the z-axis.

B. Force is a vector, which means there must be a direction associated with the force. Since the magnetic force is a cross-product, a mathematical vector operation, of the velocity and the magnetic field, the *Right-Hand Rule* can be used to determine the direction of the magnetic force on a positive charge.

1. Holding your right hand out, extend your index finger, hold your thumb straight up, and bend your middle finger such that it is perpendicular to your index finger, pointing away from your palm. Curl your ring finger and pinky into your palm.

2. Your index finger points in the direction of the velocity, your middle finger represents the magnetic field direction, and your thumb is the magnetic force, as shown in Figure 11.1 below.

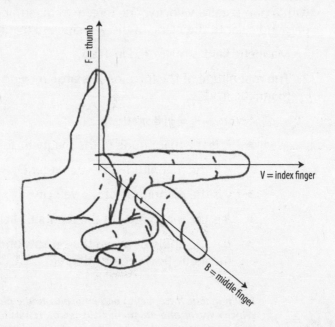

Figure 11.1

Test Tip

There are several versions of the Right-Hand Rule, all of which give the same result.

C. A negatively charged particle will be forced in the opposite direction as a positive charge.

Test Tip *When answering a question about a negative charge, determine what a positive charge would do and then give the opposite answer for the negative charge.*

D. Since a current is essentially a bunch of charges moving, a current-carrying wire also experiences a force in a magnetic field.

1. Current is

$$I = \frac{Q}{t}$$

The total charge passing a point is:

$$Q = It$$

The magnetic force is:

$$F_B = qvB \sin \theta$$

Substituting for q:

$$F_B = ItvB \sin \theta$$

Distance is vt:

$$d = vt$$

The distance the charge moves is equivalent to the length of the wire:

$$d = l$$

Therefore, the force on the current carrying wire is:

$$F_B = ILB \sin \theta$$

➤ F_B is the magnitude of the magnetic force, N

➤ I is the current in the wire, A

➤ L is the length of the wire, m

➤ B is the magnitude of the magnetic field, T

➤ θ is the angle between the current and the magnetic field, degrees

4. The direction of the magnetic force on a current-carrying wire can be determined using the same Right-Hand Rule for positive charges. Conventional current is the direction that positive charges would move, the current is the equivalent of the velocity.

II. APPLICATIONS OF MAGNETIC FIELDS

A. Since the magnetic force is always perpendicular to the velocity of the charge, the magnetic force is *centripetal*.

B. The magnetic force is providing the centripetal force.

C. When the angle between the velocity and the magnetic field is 90 degrees, the path is circular.

D. When the angle between the velocity and the magnetic field is less than 90 degrees, the path is a helix.

E. The mass-spectrometer uses this predictable circular path as a method for determining the mass of charged particles.

$$F_B = F_C$$

$$qvB = \frac{mv^2}{r}$$

$$qB = \frac{mv}{r}$$

F. A charged particle experiences a force due to an electric field. Combining an electric field and magnetic field can result in a charged particle moving in a straight line.

1. If the electric force is balanced by the magnetic force, then the charged particle moves through the region with no deflection.

$$F_E = F_B$$

$$qE = qvB$$

$$E = vB$$

$$v = \frac{E}{B}$$

2. This result is referred to as a *velocity selector*.

3. The speed the particle needs to move straight is the ratio of the electric field strength to the magnetic field strength.

III. **MAGNETIC FIELD CREATED BY A CURRENT-CARRYING WIRE**

A. Experimentally it was discovered that a current-carrying wire creates a magnetic field.

B. The magnetic field created by a long straight conductor forms concentric circles around the wire.

1. The right-hand rule for the magnetic field around a wire follows that the thumb of the right hand points in the direction of the conventional current. The fingers of the right hand then curl around the wire denoting the direction of the magnetic field in the concentric circles surrounding the wire.

2. Experimentally it was determined that the magnetic-field strength decreases as the distance from the conductor increases, yet it increases as the magnitude of the current increases.

3. The equation for the magnetic field at a distance from a long straight conductor obeys Ampere's Law:

$$B = \frac{\mu_o I}{2\pi r}$$

➤ *B* is the magnetic field strength, *T*

➤ μ_o is the permeability of free space, $4\pi \times 10^{-7} \frac{Tm}{A}$

➤ *I* is the current in the conductor, *A*

➤ *r* is the distance from the conductor, *m*

Test Tip "Into the page" *is denoted by X's and* "out of the page" *is denoted by •'s.*

IV. MAGNETIC FORCE BETWEEN TWO CURRENT-CARRYING CONDUCTORS

1. A current-carrying conductor creates a magnetic field, and when placed near a second current-carrying conductor, each will apply force to the other.

2. The force applied to each conductor also obeys Newton's 3rd Law of Motion—the force on each wire is equal in magnitude and opposite in direction.

3. In the case of two current-carrying conductors with current in the same direction (as shown in Figure 11.2(a)),

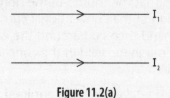

Figure 11.2(a)

I_1, creates a magnetic field directed into the page below it (as shown in Figure 11.2(b)).

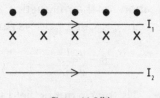

Figure 11.2(b)

Using the right-hand rule for the force on a current-carrying wire, I_2, is directed right and the magnetic field is into the page, which applies a force on I_2 directed up, as shown in Figure 11.2(c).

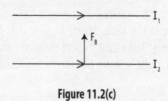

Figure 11.2(c)

Similarly, I_2 creates a magnetic field directed out of the page above it as determined by the right-hand rule for the magnetic field around a current-carrying wire (shown in Figure 11.2(d)).

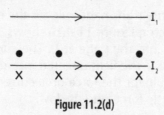

Figure 11.2(d)

The current in I_1 is directed right, according to the right-hand rule for the force on a current-carrying wire, the current is to the right and the magnetic field is out of the page. The magnetic force on I_1 is directed down (as shown in Figure 11.2(e)).

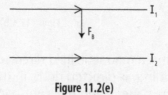

Figure 11.2(e)

Therefore, conductors carrying current in the same direction will attract one another (as shown in Figure 11.3).

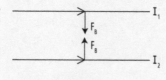

Figure 11.3

4. Similarly, the force between two conductors with currents in the opposite direction, Figure 11.4(a), can be determined by applying the right-hand rule for the magnetic force acting on a conductor in a magnetic field.

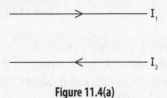

Figure 11.4(a)

Using the right-hand rule for the magnetic field created by a conductor, Figure 11.4(b) shows the magnetic field created by I_1 is into the page at I_2. The current in I_2 is directed left, in a magnetic field directed into the page. Using the right-hand rule for the force on a current-carrying wire, the magnetic force on I_2 is down.

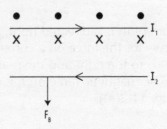

Figure 11.4(b)

I_2 creates a magnetic field directed into the page at I_1. The current in I_1 is directed right, in the magnetic field directed into the page. Using the right-hand rule for the force on a current carrying wire, the magnetic force is up, as shown in Figure 11.4(c)

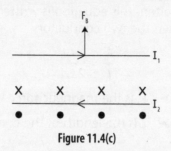

Figure 11.4(c)

Therefore, conductors carrying current in the opposite direction will repel one another, as shown in Figure 11.4(d).

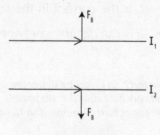

Figure 11.4(d)

Currents in the same direction apply an attractive force.
Currents in the opposite direction apply a repulsive force.

5. The force on I_2 due to the magnetic field of I_1 can be calculated by:

$$F_B = I_2 L B_1$$

Where $B_1 = \dfrac{\mu_0 I_1}{2\pi r}$ is the magnetic field created by I_1, the result is:

$$F_B = I_2 L \left(\dfrac{\mu_0 I_1}{2\pi r} \right)$$

Most often, this equation is written as the *force per length* between the two conductors.

$$\frac{F_B}{L} = \frac{\mu_o I_2 I_1}{2\pi d}$$

➤ F_B is the magnetic force on the conductor, N

➤ L is the length of the conductor, m

➤ μ_o is the permeability of free space, $4\pi \times 10^{-7} \frac{Tm}{A}$

➤ I_1 is the current in the conductor (1), A

➤ I_2 is the current in the conductor (2), A

➤ d is the distance between the conductors, m

Test Tip

The force on I_1 can be determined using the same method, which will conclude that the magnitude of the forces on each wire is the same, further supporting Newton's 3rd Law of Motion.

V. MAGNETIC FLUX

A. *Flux* comes from the Latin word for *flow*. *Magnetic flux* is a scalar quantity that describes the amount of magnetic field that passes through an area perpendicular to the magnetic field lines.

B. Figure 11.5 below shows the magnetic field passing through the area of a hoop.

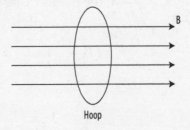

Hoop

Figure 11.5

C. Magnetic flux is at maximum when the angle between the magnetic field lines and the normal to the plane of the area is 0°, as shown in Figure 11.6.

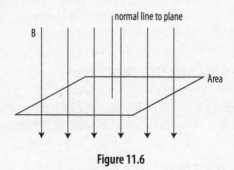

Figure 11.6

D. Magnetic flux is at minimum when the angle between the magnetic field lines and the normal line to the plane of the area is 90°, as shown in Figure 11.7.

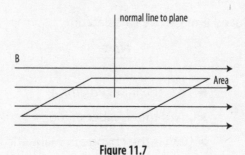

Figure 11.7

E. The magnetic flux can be calculated using:

$$\Phi = BA \cos \theta$$

➤ Φ is the magnetic flux, *Wb*

➤ *B* is the magnetic field, *T*

➤ *A* is the area, *m²*

➤ θ is the angle between the magnetic field lines and the normal to the plane of the area

Test Tip

Magnetic flux is measured in **Weber (Wb)** *which is equivalent to Tm²·*

VI. ELECTROMAGNETIC INDUCTION

A. Faraday's Law of Induction states that a change in magnetic flux over time induces a voltage across a conductor, *induced emf* .

1. A loop created by a conductor serves as the area.

2. The changing magnetic field creates relative motion between the magnetic field and the free charges in the conductor. The relative motion results in a force on each of the charges. The result of the motion is current.

B. Induced emf can be calculated:

$$\varepsilon = \frac{N\Delta\Phi}{\Delta t}$$

➤ ε is the induced emf, V

➤ N is the number of loops

➤ $\Delta\Phi$ is the change in magnetic flux, Tm^2

➤ Δt is the time during which the change in flux occurred, s

1. An induced emf is created if there is a change in magnetic flux.

2. A change in magnetic flux may occur due to a change in magnetic field strength, an increase or decrease in magnitude.

3. A change in magnetic flux may occur due to a change in the area enclosed by the conductor, an increase or decrease in the size of area.

4. A change in magnetic flux may occur due to a change in the angle between the magnetic field and the normal line to the plane of the area, a rotation of the loop about an axis is perpendicular to the magnetic field.

D. Lenz's law states that the induced current in a conductor flows in a direction to produce a magnetic field to oppose the change in magnetic flux that induced the emf.

1. A conducting loop, shown in Figure 11.8(a), is initially isolated.

   i. A magnetic flux is created through the loop when an external magnetic field is introduced, Figure 11.8(b).

   ii. The magnetic flux in the area of the loop is *increasing* into the page.

   iii. The conductor creates a magnetic field *out* of the page.

   iv. Use the right-hand rule for the magnetic field around a wire. The thumb of the right hand indicates a counter-clockwise current in the conductor, as shown in Figure 11.8(c).

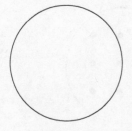
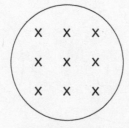
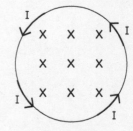

Figure 11.8(a)   Figure 11.8(b)   Figure 11.8(c)

2. A conducting loop, shown in Figure 11.9, is initially in an external magnetic field.

   i. When removed from the magnetic field, the wire sets up a magnetic field in the same direction.

   ii. Use the right-hand rule for the magnetic field created by a wire. The thumb of the right hand indicates a clockwise current.

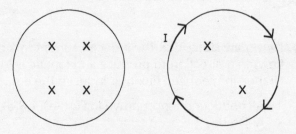

Figure 11.9

3. Alternately, when the external magnetic field is in the *opposite* direction, the current is also in the opposite direction.

4. Figure 11.10(a) shows an isolated conductor. An external magnetic field, directed out of the page is added to the loop, inducing a clockwise current, as shown in Figure 11.10(b).

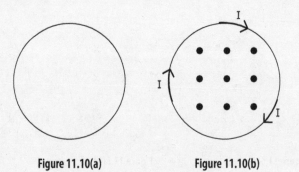

Figure 11.10(a)   **Figure 11.10(b)**

5. Figure 11.10(c) shows a conductor in an external magnetic field directed out of the page. As the magnetic field decreases, the magnetic flux decreases *out* of the page. The conductor responds by creating a magnetic field also directed out of the page resulting in a counter-clockwise current, as shown in Figure 11.10(d).

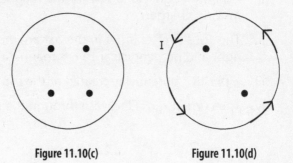

Figure 11.10(c)   Figure 11.10(d)

E. *Motional emf* is a term used to describe the induced emf created by the motion of a bar sliding along conducting rails, as shown in Figure 11.11.

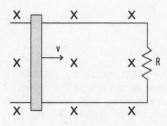

Figure 11.11

1. As the bar moves through the magnetic field, the charges inside the bar are also moving perpendicular to the magnetic field.

2. Positive and negative charges are forced in opposite directions in a magnetic field, creating a potential difference across the bar.

3. The potential difference across the bar is then applied to the conducting rails that have a resistance denoted by the resistor in Figure 11.11. The result is an induced current.

4. In the case shown in Figure 11.12, the bar is moving to the right in the magnetic field directed into the page.

  i.   Using the right-hand rule for the magnetic force on a moving charge.

  ii. The "positive" charges in the bar are moving to the right and perpendicular to the magnetic field.

  iii. A positive potential is created at the top of the bar.

  iv. The current runs clockwise through the external circuit.

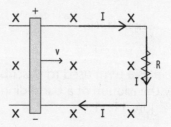

Figure 11.12

The direction of the current in Figure 11.12 can be confirmed using Lenz's Law. The amount of magnetic field inside the loop is decreasing; the wire will create a magnetic field in the same direction to make up for the loss. Fingers of the right hand will point into the page inside the loop; grab the wire. The thumb points in a direction denoting a clockwise current anywhere along the loop.

F. The motional emf can be calculated starting with Faraday's Law:

$$|\varepsilon| = \frac{N\Delta\Phi}{\Delta t}$$

The change in magnetic flux is due to the change in the area enclosed by the circuit:

$$\Delta\Phi = B\Delta A \cos\theta$$

In this case, the area enclosed by the loop is decreasing as the bar moves to the right, perpendicular to the magnetic field (Figure 11.13).

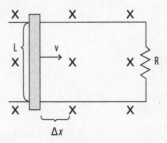

Figure 11.13

The decrease in area is $\Delta A = L\Delta x$.

Substituting the ΔA expression back into the changing magnetic flux equation:

$$\Delta\Phi = B(L\Delta x) \cos 90$$

Substituting the $\Delta\Phi$ expression back into the induced emf equation:

$$|\varepsilon| = \frac{B(L\Delta x)}{\Delta t}$$

Where $\dfrac{\Delta x}{\Delta t} = v$

$$|\varepsilon| = BLv$$

➤ ε is motional emf, V

➤ B is the magnetic field, T

➤ L is the length of the bar, m

➤ v is the speed of the bar, $\dfrac{m}{s}$

PART V

WAVES
AND
OPTICS

Oscillations and Waves

I. OSCILLATIONS: MASS ON SPRING AND MASS ON A STRING (PENDULUM)

A. Both springs and pendulums exhibit *Simple Harmonic Motion.*

B. Simple Harmonic Motion (SHM) is defined as periodic motion that occurs due to a restoring force.

C. A restoring force is one that points towards the equilibrium position and is directly proportional to the displacement from equilibrium.

D. A mass oscillating on a spring resting on a frictionless horizontal surface exhibits wave-like motion.

1. In the horizontal arrangement shown in Figure 12.1(a), the mass is initially displaced a distance (A) from the equilibrium position, $x = 0$. When released at the maximum displacement, the acceleration of the mass is at maximum, $F = ma = -kx$. The spring force is the *restoring force.*

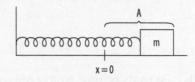

Figure 12.1(a)

2. When released, the mass will move to the left, passing through the equilibrium position, as shown in Figure 12.1(b). At the equilibrium position, the velocity of the mass is at a maximum and the acceleration is at a minimum ($a = 0$).

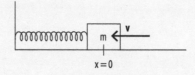

Figure 12.1(b)

3. The mass then begins to slow down as the spring is compressed on the left side of the equilibrium position. The mass stops momentarily at $-A$, as shown in Figure 12.1(c). The acceleration is again at a maximum.

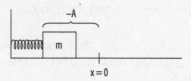

Figure 12.1(c)

4. The mass then passes back though the equilibrium position, again moving at a maximum velocity, as shown in Figure 12.1(d).

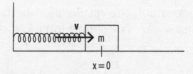

Figure 12.1(d)

5. Finally, the mass returns to the original position, A, and momentarily stops, but has reached a maximum acceleration once again, as shown in Figure 12.1(e).

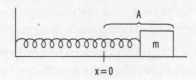

Figure 12.1(e)

6. The position of the mass as it moves along the horizontal surface can be translated into a wave pattern, as shown in Figure 12.2. The mass is initially at a positive maximum position. It speeds up as it passes through the equilibrium position and slows down as it approaches the maximum negative displacement.

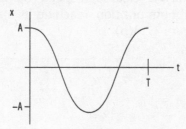

Figure 12.2

7. From the graph of the position of the mass as a function of time, the velocity as a function of time, Figure 12.3(a), and the acceleration as a function of time, Figure 12.3(b), can be created as shown below.

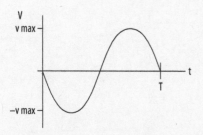

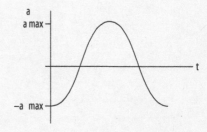

Figure 12.3(a)   **Figure 12.3(b)**

C. A mass oscillating on a vertical spring, with no frictional forces acting upon it, exhibits wave-like motion.

1. Figure 12.4(a) shows a mass compressed on a vertical spring, above the equilibrium position.

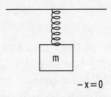

$-x = 0$

Figure 12.4(a)

2. The mass is released; it speeds up as it passes through the equilibrium position, reaching its maximum speed, as shown in Figure 12.4(b)

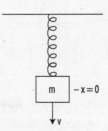

$-x = 0$

v

Figure 12.4(b)

3. The mass begins to slow until it stops momentarily, as shown in Figure 12.4(c).

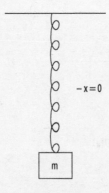

$-x = 0$

Figure 12.4(c)

4. The mass will then return back to the original position, as shown in Figure 12.4(a). This resulting motion can be translated into a wave pattern, as shown in Figure 12.5. The mass is initially at a positive maximum position. It speeds up as it passes through the equilibrium position and slows down as it approaches the maximum negative displacement.

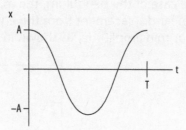

Figure 12.5

D. A pendulum swinging through very small angular displacements exhibits wave-like motion.

1. The restoring force for a pendulum is the component of the weight pointing towards the lowest point in the swing, as shown in Figure 12.6.

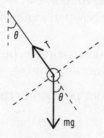

Figure 12.6

2. The restoring force is:

$$F_{restore} = mg \sin \theta$$

As defined in SHM, the restoring force is directly proportional to the displacement. For a pendulum, the displacement is the angle. For a pendulum to exhibit true SHM, the angle must be very small.

3. In the case of the pendulum, the maximum displacement is the linear displacement from the equilibrium position to the max or min amplitude, as shown in Figure 12.7.

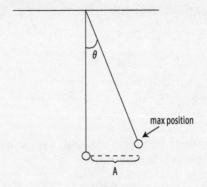

Figure 12.7

4. The resulting motion can be translated into the same wave pattern, as shown in Figure 12.6.

E. The equations for maximum position, x, maximum velocity, v, and maximum acceleration, a, are as follows:

1. The maximum position occurs when $\omega t = 0$, therefore:

$$x_{max} = A$$

➤ x is position, m

➤ A is amplitude, m

2. The maximum velocity occurs when $\omega t = 90°$, therefore:

$$v_{max} = A\omega$$

➤ v is velocity, $\dfrac{m}{s}$

➤ A is amplitude, m

➤ ω is angular speed/frequency, $\dfrac{radians}{s}$

3. The maximum acceleration occurs when $\omega t = 0$, therefore:

$$a_{max} = A\omega^2$$

➤ a is acceleration, $\dfrac{m}{s^2}$

➤ A is amplitude, m

➤ ω is angular speed/frequency, $\dfrac{radians}{s}$

F. Simple harmonic motion is periodic. The period can be derived from setting the maximum restoring force equal to ma_{max}:

1. For the spring:

$$kx = mA\omega^2$$

Where $x_{max} = A$

$$kA = mA\omega^2$$

Which reduces to

$$k = m\omega^2$$

Therefore,

$$\omega = \sqrt{\dfrac{k}{m}}$$

Thus the angular frequency depends on the spring constant and the mass of the object.

2. Angular speed/frequency for one complete revolution/cycle can be written as:

$$\omega = \frac{2\pi}{T}$$

Substitution for the angular speed:

$$\sqrt{\frac{k}{m}} = \frac{2\pi}{T}$$

Rearranging gives the period as:

$$T = 2\pi\sqrt{\frac{m}{k}}$$

➤ *T* is period, *s*

➤ *m* is mass, *kg*

➤ *k* is the spring constant, $\frac{N}{m}$

3. For the pendulum:

$$mg\ sin\ \theta = mA\omega^2$$

Where $A = l\ sin\ \theta$ (for small angles) from the geometry of Figure 12.7.

$$mg\ sin\ \theta = ml\ sin\ \theta\ \omega^2$$

This reduces to

$$g = L\omega^2$$

Therefore,

$$\omega = \sqrt{\frac{g}{L}}$$

Thus, the angular speed/frequency depends on the acceleration of gravity on the planet and the length of the pendulum.

4. Angular speed/frequency for one complete revolution/cycle can be written as:

$$\omega = \frac{2\pi}{T}$$

Substitution for the angular speed:

$$\sqrt{\frac{g}{L}} = \frac{2\pi}{T}$$

Rearranging gives the period as:

$$T = 2\pi\sqrt{\frac{L}{g}}$$

➤ T is period, s

➤ L is length, m

➤ g is the acceleration of gravity at the location of the pendulum, $\frac{m}{s^2}$

G. The energy stored in a spring or pendulum is transformed into kinetic energy when released from a non-equilibrium position.

1. For springs:

$$-\Delta U_s = \Delta K$$

$$-\left(\frac{1}{2}kx^2 - \frac{1}{2}kx_o^2\right) = \left(\frac{1}{2}mv^2 - \frac{1}{2}mv_o^2\right)$$

Which commonly reduces to:

$$\frac{1}{2}kx_{max}^2 = \frac{1}{2}mv_{max}^2$$

If $x_o = x_{max}$ and $v = v_{max}$

2. For pendulums:

$$-\Delta U_g = \Delta K$$

$$-(mgy - mgy_o) = \left(\frac{1}{2}mv^2 - \frac{1}{2}mv_o^2\right)$$

Which commonly reduces to:

$$mgy_{max} = \frac{1}{2}mv_{max}^2$$

If $y_o = y_{max}$ and $v = v_{max}$

Test Tip

The height of a pendulum's mass above the equilibrium position can be determined geometrically to be $y = L - L \cos \theta$.

II. WAVES

A. A wave can be defined as a disturbance that transfers energy from one location to another.

B. There are four basic properties of waves:

1. Amplitude, A—the maximum displacement from the equilibrium position, m

2. Frequency, f—how often the wave passes a fixed point, Hertz (Hz)

3. Period, T—the time it takes for one wave to pass a fixed point, s

4. Wavelength, λ—the distance between consecutive points on a wave, m.

C. The major characteristics of a wave are shown below in Figure 12.8:

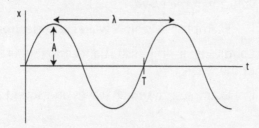

Figure 12.8

D. The frequency of a wave is indirectly proportional to the period of the wave.

$$f = \frac{1}{T}$$

➤ *f* is frequency, Hz

➤ *T* is period, *s*

E. The speed of a wave can be calculated by:

$$v = f\lambda$$

➤ *v* is velocity, $\frac{m}{s}$

➤ *f* is frequency, Hz

➤ λ is wavelength, *m*

Test Tip

The speed and frequency equations hold true for all types of waves—mechanical waves and electromagnetic waves.

F. The two types of waves are:

1. Transverse—the disturbance moves perpendicular to the velocity of the wave.

    i. Examples: seismic S waves and electromagnetic waves

2. Longitudinal—the disturbance moves parallel to the velocity of the wave.

    i. Examples: seismic P waves and sound waves.

G. When a wave encounters a boundary, it can be *reflected* and/or *refracted*.

1. Reflection of a wave occurs when the wave bounces off a boundary. It can be *in-phase* or *out of phase*.

    i. An in-phase reflection occurs when the wave bounces off the boundary and has the same orientation as the incoming wave (shown in Figure 12.9).

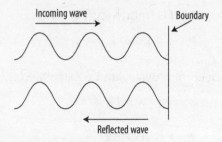

Figure 12.9

In-phase reflection occurs when:

➤ electromagnetic waves strike a boundary with lower density

➤ sound waves strike a boundary with a lower density

➤ a wave on a string is attached to a fixed point/ boundary

ii. An out-of-phase reflection occurs with the wave bounces off the boundary and has the exact opposite orientation as the incoming wave (shown in Figure 12.10).

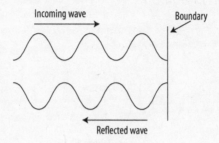

Incoming wave →   Boundary

← Reflected wave

Figure 12.10

Out-of-phase reflection occurs when:

➤ electromagnetic waves strike a boundary with higher density.

➤ sound waves strike a boundary with a higher density.

➤ a wave on a string is unattached.

iii. Refraction occurs when the wave encounters a boundary and changes speed. The change in speed causes the wave to bend.

H. When the wave encounters an opening or slit that is small, the wave bends. The bending of the waves is called *diffraction*, as shown in Figure 12.11.

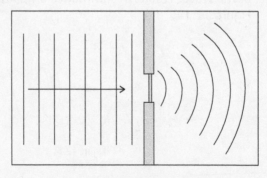

Figure 12.11

I. As two or more waves pass through the same position at the same time, the waves are added together, or superimposed. The result is superposition. An example of superposition is shown in Figure 12.12.

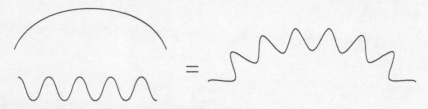

Figure 12.12

J. When two or more waves are continuously superimposed, a new wave pattern is created. The result is *interference*.

   1. Destructive interference occurs when the superposition of the waves results in zero amplitude, as shown in Figure 12.13.

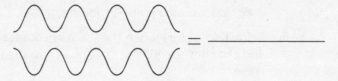

Figure 12.13

   2. Constructive interference occurs when the superposition of the waves results in summative amplitude, as shown in Figure 12.14.

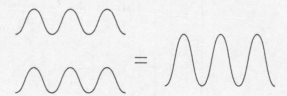

Figure 12.14

III. SOUND

A. When air particles vibrate inside a pipe, an interference pattern is created for specific frequencies. This wave pattern is called a *standing* wave, as it appears not to move.

B. A standing wave formed on a string fixed on both ends (as shown in Figure 12.15) contains two nodes (one at each end) and an anti-node (in the middle). This is the simplest standing wave that can be formed in this string; it is referred to as the *fundamental*.

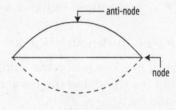

Figure 12.15

1. At any time, the string is either at or between the maximum or minimum positions.

2. The fundamental frequency, or first harmonic, is the frequency needed to create the standing wave pattern in Figure 12.15.

3. The next three possible frequencies, or harmonics, are shown in Figure 12.16.

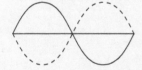 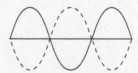 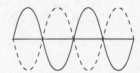

Figure 12.16

    i. Nodes are always at the fixed end.

    ii. Nodes and anti-nodes alternate along the wave pattern.

    iii. The number of "loops" indicates the number of the harmonic. Figure 12.16(a) shows the 2nd, 3rd, and 4th harmonics.

    iv. The frequency of the wave in the string can be calculated by:

$$f_n = \frac{nv}{2L}$$

➤ *f* is the frequency, Hz

➤ *n* is the number of the harmonic (1,2,3,...)

➤ *v* is the speed of the wave on the string, $\frac{m}{s}$

➤ *L* is the length of the string, *m*

4. The speed of the wave on the string depends on the mass/length of the string and the tension in the string and can be calculated by:

$$v = \sqrt{\frac{T}{\mu}}$$

➤ *v* is the speed of the wave on the string, $\frac{m}{s}$

➤ *T* is the tension in the string, N

➤ μ is the mass/length of the string, $\frac{kg}{m}$

C. A standing wave created in a pipe open on both ends is shown in Figure 12.17.

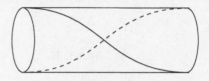

Figure 12.17

Sound waves are longitudinal, but most often the waves in the pipe are drawn as transverse waves. This is due to the difficulty in drawing longitudinal waves.

1. A displacement anti-node is created at the open end of a pipe. This is due to the unchanging atmospheric pressure at the end of the pipe.

2. The frequency of the wave created in the open pipe can be calculated by:

$$f_n = \frac{nv}{2L}$$

> ➤ *f* is the frequency, Hz

> ➤ *n* is the number of the harmonic (1,2,3,...)

> ➤ *v* is the speed of sound in the medium in the pipe, $\frac{m}{s}$

> ➤ *L* is the length of the pipe, *m*

Commonly, air is the medium in the pipe. Therefore v represents the speed of sound in air.

3. The next three harmonics in the open pipe are shown in Figure 12.18.

  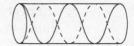

Figure 12.18

4. Figure 12.18 shows the 2nd, 3rd, and 4th harmonics.

D. A standing wave in an open/closed pipe is shown in Figure 12.19.

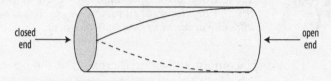

closed end → ← open end

Figure 12.19

1. A node is formed at the closed end and a displacement anti-node is formed at the open end.

2. The frequency of the wave created in the open pipe can be calculated by:

$$f_n = \frac{nv}{4L}$$

➤ f is the frequency, Hz

➤ n is the number of the harmonic (1,3,5...)

➤ v is the speed of sound in the medium in the pipe, $\frac{m}{s}$

➤ L is the length of the pipe, m

Test Tip

The open/closed pipe only forms odd harmonics. This is due to the asymmetrical nature of the standing waves formed in the pipe.

3. The next three harmonics in the open/closed pipe are shown in Figure 12.20.

 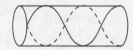 

Figure 12.20(a)   **Figure 12.20(b)**   **Figure 12.20(c)**

➤ Figure 12.20 (a), (b), and (c) show the third, fifth, and seventh harmonics, respectively.

E. The Doppler Effect describes the phenomenon observed as a sound source is moving relative to the observer.

1. The relative motion between the source and the observer affects the frequency observed.

2. When the relative motion is toward each other, the observed frequency is higher.

3. When the relative motion is away from each other, the observed frequency is lower.

Light and Optics

I. PHYSICAL OPTICS

A. Light diffracts or bends as it passes through an opening. The bending causes a disruption in the wave pattern. The waves interfere and create patterns of light.

    1. Interference occurs when monochromatic light falls on a double slit apparatus (usually referred to as Young's Double Slit). The same pattern is formed when two identical light sources are placed close together. A pattern of bright and dark fringes is created, as shown in Figure 13.1.

Figure 13.1

    2. Constructive interference occurs when the amplitudes of the light waves cross, resulting in a *bright* fringe.

    3. Destructive interference occurs when a positive amplitude and a negative amplitude cross, resulting in a *dark* fringe.

    4. The amplitude of the light waves can be represented by lines, as shown in Figure 13.2.

All waves exhibit interference. Therefore, two sound sources of equal frequency will create a similar interference pattern.

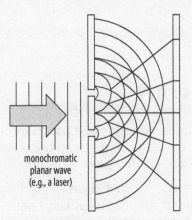

monochromatic
planar wave
(e.g., a laser)

(Note: The separation distance between the two slits
is much smaller than the distance to the screen.)

Figure 13.2

i.   The positions where the lines cross are instances of constructive interference. The bright fringes are located by following those lines to the screen. Between the light fringes are the dark fringes.

ii. The distance between each bright fringe is constant.

iii. The central bright is labeled $m = 0$, with the bright fringes above and below labeled $m = 1$ and $m = -1$, respectively. The succeeding fringes are labeled $m = \pm 2$, ± 3, ...

iv. If the distance between the slits is much smaller than the distance between the slits and the screen, as shown in Figure 13.3, the distance from the central bright fringe to the mth bright fringe can be found by:

$$\tan\theta = \frac{y}{L}$$

➤ θ is the angle between L and the line connecting the center point of the slit openings to the mth bright fringe

➤ y is the distance from the central bright to the mth bright fringe, m

➤ L is the distance from the slits to the screen, m

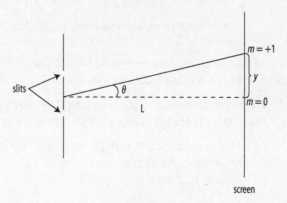

Figure 13.3

v. The difference in distance from each opening to the screen represents the *path difference* between the waves, as shown in Figure 13.4. In order for the waves to constructively interfere, the path difference must be equal to a whole integer of the wavelength.

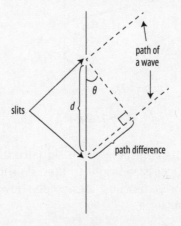

Figure 13.4

vi. The path difference can be calculated by:

$$d \sin \theta = m\lambda$$

➤ d is the slit separation, m

➤ θ is the angle between the slit and the perpendicular line, degrees

➤ $m = 0, \pm1, \pm2, \pm3 \ldots$ for bright fringes

➤ λ is the wavelength of the monochromatic light, m

B. Interference occurs as monochromatic light passes through a single slit (or a Fraunhofer Single Slit).

1. As monochromatic light is incident on the opening, the light wave bends and produces an interference pattern.

i. The central bright is most intense. The subsequent bright fringes decrease in intensity, as shown in Figure 13.5(a).

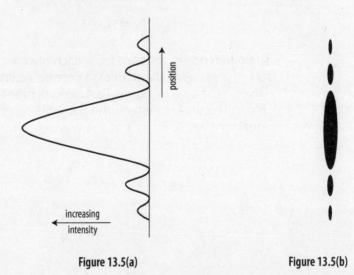

Figure 13.5(a)   **Figure 13.5(b)**

ii. The central bright is significantly larger than the successive bright fringes. As shown in Figure 13.5(b), the pattern on the screen shows a much larger central maxima.

    ii.   The width of the opening can be calculated by:

$$d \sin \theta = m\lambda$$

➤ *d* is the slit width, *m*

➤ *θ* is the angle between the slit opening and the perpendicular line, degrees

➤ *m* = ±1, ±2, ±3… for dark fringes. There is a central maximum for *m* = 0.

➤ *λ* is the wavelength of the monochromatic light, *m*

2. A diffraction grating creates an interference pattern due to the number of slits per length.

    i.   The pattern is the summation of many single slit interference patterns arranged very closely to one another.

    ii.   The distance between each slit can be found by:

$$d \sin \theta = m\lambda$$

➤ *d* is the distance between slits, *m*

➤ *θ* is the angle between the slit and the perpendicular line, degrees

➤ *m* = 0, ±1, ±2, ±3… for bright fringes

➤ *λ* is the wavelength of the monochromatic light, *m*

    iii.   Most diffraction gratings are labeled by the *number of lines per length.* The lines per length can be calculated by:

$$N = \frac{1}{d}$$

➤ *N* is the number of lines per length, m^{-1}

➤ *d* is the distance between each slit, *m*

3. Thin film interference is one of the most commonly observed instances of interference. This can be seen in the rainbow pattern on a soap bubble, CD, or DVD.

i. In Figure 13.6, Ray 1 strikes the surface of a thin film.

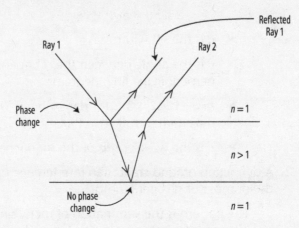

Figure 13.6

ii. Ray 1 is reflected from the surface of the film and refracted into the film, which is then reflected from the boundary and refracted back into the air as Ray 2.

iii. The result of the interference between reflected Ray 1 and Ray 2 creates a pattern, often a rainbow.

iv. The pattern created is a predictable pattern, where the position of the dark fringe can be calculated using:

$$m = \frac{2nt}{\lambda_{vacuum}}$$

➤ m is the dark fringe number

➤ n is the index of refraction of the thin film

➤ t is the thickness of the film, m

➤ λ_{vacuum} is the wavelength of light in a vacuum, m

C. Light reflects and refracts at the boundary between two media.

1. The speed of light can be calculated by:

    $$v = f\lambda$$

    ➤ v is the speed of light, $\frac{m}{s}$

    ➤ f is the frequency, Hz

    ➤ λ is the wavelength, m

2. The speed of light in a vacuum is nearly $c = 3 \times 10^8 \frac{m}{s}$.

3. The speed of light in a medium depends on the index of refraction of the material.

    i.   The index of refraction is a ratio of the speed of light in a vacuum to the speed of light in the material.

    $$n = \frac{c}{v}$$

    ➤ n is the index of refraction

    ➤ c is the speed of light in a vacuum, $3 \times 10^8 \frac{m}{s}$

4. As light passes from one material to another, the frequency remains constant. The wavelength and speed change.

5. The degree to which the light bends depends on the index of refraction of the material.

    i.   The angle to which the light bends depends on the angle of incidence and the indices of refraction. The angle of refraction can be calculated by Snell's Law:

    $$n_1 \sin \theta_1 = n_2 \sin \theta_2$$

    ➤ n is the index of refraction of the material

    ➤ θ is the angle between the normal to the surface and the ray

ii. The table below shows the path of a ray as it passes through a boundary.

Diagrams	Explanation
θ_1 n_1 $n_1 < n_2$ n_2 θ_2	$n_1 < n_2$ The light is going from a low index of refraction to a high index of refraction. The refracted ray will bend towards the normal line.
θ_1 $n_1 < n_2$ θ_2	$n_1 > n_2$ The light is going from a high index of refraction to a low index of refraction. The refracted ray will bend away from the normal line.
θ_1 n_1 n_2 θ_2	$n_1 = n_2$ The light is not refracted because the materials have the same index of refraction.

6. Total internal reflection occurs when the light inside a material is reflected back into the material.

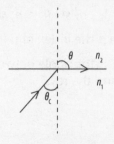

Figure 13.7

i.   Figure 13.7 shows the minimum case. The refracted ray, θ, must be at least 90°. When applied to Snell's Law, the equation reduces to:

$$\theta_C = \sin^{-1}\frac{n_1}{n_2}$$

   ➤ θ_C is the critical angle, degrees

   ➤ n_2 is the index of refraction the material creating the boundary

   ➤ n_1 is the index of refraction of the material in which the light originates

ii. The critical angle is the minimum angle needed to create total internal reflection. Any angle greater than θ_C results in a reflected ray equal to that of the incident ray.

iii. Total internal reflection can only occur if the light is going from a high index of refraction to a low index of refraction.

7. Dispersion occurs when light passes through a medium and the wavelengths of light are separated.

i.   Each wavelength of light has a specific index of refraction; blue light has a higher index of refraction and bends more than red light.

ii. Prisms are used to create dispersion, as shown in Figure 13.8.

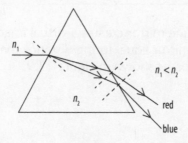

Figure 13.8

      iii. If the incident ray is white light, the different wavelengths of light bend at different angles. This results in a rainbow.

D. Mirrors use reflection and lenses use refraction to create images.

   1. There are two types of images formed: *real* and *virtual.*

      i. Real images are formed when refracted rays actually form the image.

        ➤ Projectable, inverted

      ii. Virtual images are formed when refracted rays appear to form the image.

        ➤ Cannot be projected, upright

   2. Magnification is the ratio of the height of the image to the height of the object, which is also equal to the ratio of the image distance to the object distance.

$$M = \frac{h_i}{h_o} = -\frac{s_i}{s_o}$$

+M	Upright, virtual image
−M	Inverted, real image
$|M| > 1$	Enlarged image
$|M| < 1$	Reduced image
$|M| = 1$	Image height equals object height

   3. A plane mirror creates a virtual image at a distance behind the mirror equal to the distance the object is in front of the mirror, as shown in Figure 13.9.

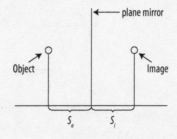

Figure 13.9

    i.   The magnification of an image in a plane mirror is +1.

4. Spherical mirrors being part of a sphere have a *radius of curvature*. The curvature creates a focal point for the light.

$$f = \frac{R}{2}$$

➤ *f* is the focal point, *m*

➤ *R* is the radius of curvature, *m*

5. A spherical mirror forms an image in a position relative to the mirror and dependent on the focal point and the object's distance from the mirror. The position of the object, image and the focal point are related by:

$$\frac{1}{s_o} + \frac{1}{s_i} = \frac{1}{f}$$

➤ s_o is the object position

➤ s_i is the image position

➤ *f* is the focal point

    i.   The sign rules for the object and image position for mirrors are:

        $+s_o$ In front of mirror

        $+s_i$ In front of mirror

        $-s_i$ Behind mirror

6. Magnification is the ratio of the height of the image to the height of the object, which is also equal to the ratio of the image distance to the object distance.

$$M = \frac{h_i}{h_o} = -\frac{d_i}{d_o}$$

$+M$	Upright, virtual image
$-M$	Inverted, real image
$\lvert M \rvert > 1$	Enlarged image
$\lvert M \rvert < 1$	Reduced image
$\lvert M \rvert = 1$	Image equal to object

7. A concave spherical mirror creates a real or virtual image. The type of image depends on the position of the object relative to the focal point.

8. A convex mirror always forms a virtual image.

9. The table below shows the relative position of an object to the focal point and its resulting image.

Concave (converging) Mirror (+f)		
As the object moves from infinity to R, the real image moves from f to R and the magnification increases from zero to 1.		$\infty > s_o > R$ $R > s_i > f$ Real image
When the object is at R, the real image is at R and the magnification is 1.		$s_o = R$ $s_i = R$ Real image

Concave (converging) Mirror (+f)		
As the object moves from R to f, the real image moves from R to infinity and increases in magnification.	Object R f Image	$R > s_o > f$ $\infty > s_i > R$ Real image
When the object is at f, no image is formed.	Object f No image	$s_o = f$ $s_i = \infty$
As the object moves from f to 0, the enlarged virtual image moves from $-\infty$ to 0 and the magnification decreases.	Object R f Image	$f > s_o > 0$ $-\infty > s_i > 0$ Virtual image

Convex (diverging) Mirror (–f)		
As the object moves from infinity to 0, the virtual image moves from –f to 0 and the magnification increases from zero to 1.		$\infty > s_o > 0$ $-f > s_i > 0$ Virtual image

10. Lenses use the difference in index of refraction to bend light and create an image.

   i. A real image is formed on the other side of the lens from the object (where the light goes).

   ii. A virtual image is formed on the same side of the lens as the object.

11. The position of the image depends on the type of lens, the focal point, and object position, relative to the lens. The thin lens equation is:

$$\frac{1}{s_o} + \frac{1}{s_i} = \frac{1}{f}$$

➤ s_o is the object position

➤ s_i is the image position

➤ f is the focal point

   i. The sign rules for the object and image position for lenses are:

$+ s_o$	In front of lens
$+ s_i$	Behind lens
$- s_i$	In front of lens

12. A converging thin lens creates a real or virtual image, depending on the position of the object relative to the focal point.

13. A diverging lens always forms a virtual image.

14. The table below shows the relative position of an object to the focal point and its resulting image.

Converging Lens (+f)		
As the object moves from infinity to 2f, the real image moves from f to 2f and the magnification increases from zero to 1.	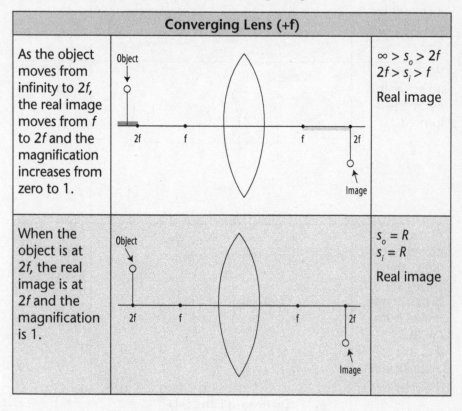	$\infty > s_o > 2f$ $2f > s_i > f$ Real image
When the object is at 2f, the real image is at 2f and the magnification is 1.		$s_o = R$ $s_i = R$ Real image

Converging Lens (+f)		
As the object moves from $2f$ to f, the real image moves from $2f$ to infinity and increases in magnification.	 Object 2f f f 2f Image	$2f > s_o > f$ $\infty > s_i > 2f$ Real image
When the object is at f, no image is formed.	 Object f f	$s_o = f$ $s_i = \infty$
As the object moves from f to 0, the enlarged virtual image moves from $-\infty$ to 0 and the magnification decreases to 1.	 Image Object f f	$f > s_o > 0$ $-\infty > s_i > 0$ Virtual image
Diverging Lens (−f)		
As the object moves from infinity to 0, the virtual image moves from f to 0 and the magnification increases from 0 to 1.	 Object Image 2f f f 2f	$\infty > s_o > 0$ $f > s_i > 0$ Virtual image

15. Ray Diagrams consist of three principal rays and are used to locate an image. The most common ray diagrams are shown below.

Concave Mirror

| **Object outside *f***
1. Dotted line—from the object, parallel to the principal axis, then reflected through the focal point.
2. Dashed line—from the object through the focal point, then reflected parallel to the principal axis.
3. Bold line—from the object, through the center of curvature, then reflected back through the center of curvature. | 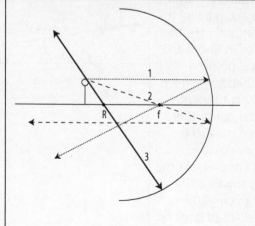 |
| **Object inside *f***
1. Dotted line—from the object, parallel to the principal axis, then reflected through the focal point.
2. Dashed line—from the object in line with the focal point, then reflected parallel to the principal axis.
3. Bold line—from the object, through the center of curvature, then reflected back through the center of curvature. | 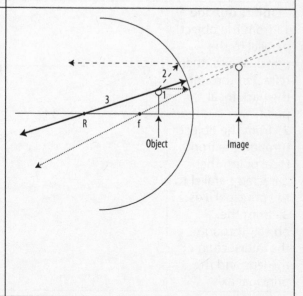 |

Convex Mirror

Object in front of mirror

1. Dotted line—from the object, parallel to the principal axis, then reflected in line with the focal point.
2. Dashed line—from the object towards the focal point, then reflected parallel to the principal axis.
3. Bold line—from the object, towards the center of curvature, then reflected back on itself.

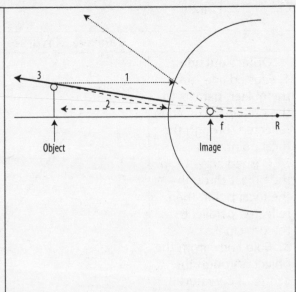

Converging Lens

Object outside *f*

1. from the object, parallel to the principal axis, then refracted through the back focal point.
2. from the object through the front focal point, then refracted parallel to the principal axis.
3. from the object, through the intersection of the lens and the principal axis.

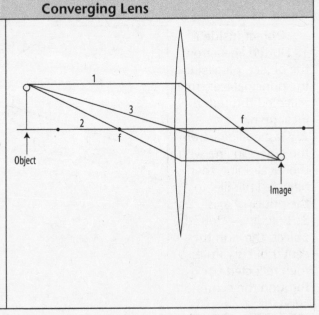

Converging Lens

Object inside *f*
1. from the object, parallel to the principal axis, then refracted through the back focal point.
2. from the object through the front focal point, then refracted parallel to the principal axis.
3. from the object, through the intersection of the lens and the principal axis.

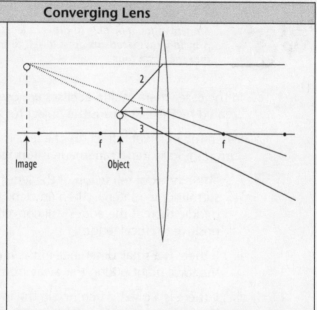

Diverging Lens

Object in front of lens
1. from the object, parallel to the principal axis, then refracted through the back focal point.
2. from the object through the front focal point, then refracted parallel to the principal axis.
3. from the object, through the intersection of the lens and the principal axis.

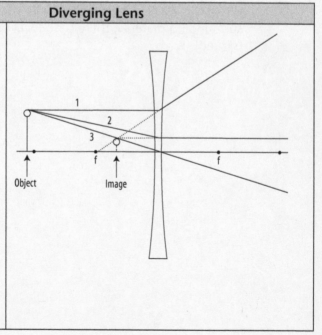

16. In the case where multiple lenses are used, the image created by the first lens is the object for the second lens.

17. When the index of refraction of a lens is different from the surrounding material, an image is formed.

    i.   If the index of refraction of the lens is greater than the surrounding material, then any lens that is thicker in the middle than at the edges will converge light, and have a positive (+) focal length.

    ii. If there is a small difference in the indices of refraction, the focal point is long (far away from the lens).

    iii. If there is a great difference in the indices of refraction, the focal point is short (close to the lens).

18. When the index of refraction of a lens is the same as the surrounding material, there is no focal point. No image is formed.

PART VI

MODERN
PHYSICS

Atomic and Nuclear Physics

PHOTONS, PHOTOELECTRIC EFFECT, X-RAY PRODUCTION, AND THE COMPTON EFFECT

A. A *photon* is a bundle of light energy and displays particle-like properties.

B. The energy of a photon depends on the frequency of the light and Planck's constant, *h*.

$$E = hf = \frac{hc}{\lambda}$$

➤ E is energy of a photon, J

➤ h is Planck's constant, 6.63×10^{-34} Js

➤ f is frequency, Hz

➤ λ is wavelength, m

➤ c is the speed of light in a vacuum, $\sim 3 \times 10^{8} \frac{m}{s}$

C. The energy of a photon can be expressed in joules or electron volts.

$$1.602 \times 10^{-19} \, J = 1 \, eV$$

1 *eV* is the energy that one charge of ±*e* gains by accelerating through a potential difference of 1 *V*.

D. Although a photon is referred to as a "particle of light," a photon has a zero rest mass but a finite momentum.

  1. The momentum of a photon can be calculated by:

$$p = \frac{hf}{c} = \frac{h}{\lambda}$$

  ➤ p is the momentum, $\dfrac{kgm}{s}$

  ➤ h is Planck's constant, 6.63×10^{-34} Js

  ➤ f is frequency, Hz

  ➤ c is the speed of light in a vacuum, $\sim 3 \times 10^8 \dfrac{m}{s}$

  ➤ λ is wavelength, m

  2. The momentum of a photon increases with increasing frequency.

Test Tip

The typical momentum of a photon is very small. For visible light, it is on the order of 10^{-27}.

E. Photons carry energy and momentum, which can be seen in the photoelectric effect, Compton scattering, and X-ray production.

F. Photoelectric effect is a quantum phenomenon that occurs when light of a minimum wavelength strikes a metal surface and an electron is ejected. A typical photoelectric device is shown in Figure 14.1.

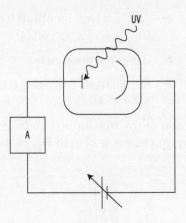

Figure 14.1

1. The minimum amount of energy needed to eject the electron is called the *work function*.

2. The maximum kinetic energy of the ejected electron is the difference in the incident photon and the work function, due to the conservation of energy.

$$K_{max} = hf - \phi$$

➤ K_{max} is the maximum kinetic energy of the ejected electron, J or eV

➤ h is Planck's constant, 6.63×10^{-34} Js or 4.14×10^{-15} eVs

➤ f is the frequency of the incident photon, Hz

➤ ϕ is the work function of the material, J or eV

3. The minimum energy the photon can have and eject an electron is the work function.

$$E_{photon} = \phi$$

4. The minimum frequency, or the *threshold frequency*, needed to eject electrons is:

$$f_{threshold} = \frac{\phi}{h}$$

➤ $f_{threshold}$ is the minimum frequency of incident light that will eject an electron, Hz

➤ ϕ is the work function, J or eV

➤ h is Planck's constant, 6.63×10^{-34} Js or 4.14×10^{-15} eVs

5. A graph of the maximum kinetic energy of the electron vs. the frequency is shown in Figure 14.2.

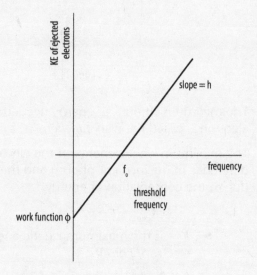

Figure 14.2

➤ The slope of the line is Planck's constant, h.

➤ Different metals have different work functions and different threshold frequencies. The graphs will be parallel because Planck's constant does not change.

6. The stream of electrons emitted from the metal surface creates a current.

7. Incident photons and ejected electrons interact on a one-to-one basis. Each electron receives the same amount of energy. Increasing the intensity of the light increases the number of photons. The number of electrons emitted increases (not the energy of each electron).

8. The current of electrons can be stopped by applying a potential difference across the gap.

   i.   The stopping potential is a reverse potential difference to slow the electron from K_{max} to 0.

   ii. The measured stopping potential is related to the kinetic energy by:

   $$K_{max} = qV$$

   ➤ The q is an electron, e = 1.602×10^{-19} C

   ➤ V is the stopping potential, V

   ➤ K_{max} is the maximum kinetic energy of an emitted electron, J

9. X-rays are produced through the following process:

   i.   Electrons are accelerated through a large potential difference, creating high energy electrons.

   ii. The high-energy electrons strike a metal target.

   iii. The electrons slow down with a very high acceleration, the electrons experience a large energy loss.

   iv. X-ray photons are produced as a result of the excitation of the electrons when bombarded by high-energy electrons.

10. The Compton Effect describes the result of a photon colliding elastically with an electron. The scattered photon has transferred some of its energy to the electron. This collision results in a lower energy photon. The photon will have a lower frequency and higher wavelength.

    i.   Employing the conservation of momentum and energy to the glancing collision results in an equation for the change in wavelength for the photon, as shown in Figure 14.3.

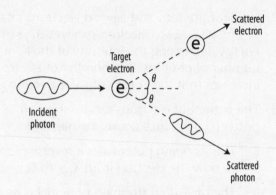

Figure 14.3

$$\Delta \lambda = \lambda' - \lambda = \frac{h}{m_e c}(1 - \cos\theta)$$

➤ $\Delta\lambda$ is the difference in the final and initial wavelengths, m

➤ λ' is the final wavelength, m

➤ λ is the initial wavelength, m

➤ h is Planck's constant, 6.63×10^{-34} Js or 4.14×10^{-15} eVs

➤ m_e is the mass of an electron, 9.11×10^{-31} kg

➤ c is the speed of light in a vacuum, $\sim 3 \times 10^8 = \frac{m}{s}$

➤ θ is the angle between the lines of the incident and scattered photons.

  ii. The maximum wavelength shift will occur when $\theta = 180°$, and is equal to $\frac{2h}{m_e c}$

11. In 1923, Louis de Broglie hypothesized that if light can behave as a particle, exhibiting energy and momentum, then matter, such as an electron, should exhibit wavelike properties. Davisson and Germer confirmed this with an experiment in which electrons scattered off of a nickel surface produced an interference pattern.

$$\lambda = \frac{h}{p}$$

➤ λ is wavelength, *m*

➤ *h* is Planck's constant, 6.63×10^{-34} *Js*

➤ *p* is the momentum, $\dfrac{kgm}{s}$

II. PHOTONS AND THE ATOM

A. The two main assumptions about electrons in an atom are:

1. The orbit is circular.

2. The electron can only orbit in specific circles.

B. Electrons orbiting the nucleus do not give off electromagnetic radiation. Electron transitions between levels involve absorbing or emitting photons.

C. When a photon with the energy equal to the energy difference between energy levels strikes an electron in an atom, the radiation is absorbed and the electron transitions to a higher energy level, as shown in Figure 14.4.

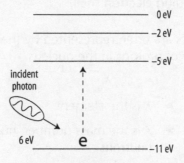

Figure 14.4

D. An electron orbiting at a higher energy state is not stable. When the electron transitions to a lower energy state, a photon of the corresponding energy difference is emitted, as shown in Figure 14.5.

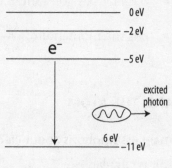

Figure 14.5

E. The process of transitioning to a lower energy level is called *spontaneous emission*. The electron decays to a lower energy state.

III. THE NUCLEUS AND NUCLEAR RADIATION

A. A nucleus contains protons and neutrons. Electrons orbit in the surrounding electron shell.

B. Elements are often represented by the mass number and the number of protons in the nucleus.

$$^A_Z X$$

➤ X is the element

➤ A is the mass number, number of protons and neutrons

➤ Z is the number of protons, or charge number

1. All nuclei of the same element have the same number of protons.

2. Nuclei of the same element with different numbers of neutrons are *isotopes*.

3. The *atomic mass unit* is a common mass conversion used to simplify the math. 1 u is defined as $\frac{1}{12}$ th the mass of a C-12 atom.

$$1u = 1.66 \times 10^{-27} \ kg$$

C. The *strong nuclear force* holds the nucleus together. The strong nuclear force only acts on proton/neutron pairs when the separation distance is very small.

1. The competition between the strong nuclear force and the electrostatic repulsive force determines the stability of the nuclei.

2. Nuclei with 20 or less neutrons are considered light and stable.

3. Nuclei with 20 to 83 neutrons are only stable if the neutrons outnumber the protons.

   i.   The additional neutrons provide more binding energy through the strong force interaction. This is necessary to counteract the increasing repulsion of the additional protons as the nuclei get larger.

5. Nuclei with more than 83 neutrons are unstable. No number of neutrons can be added to create stability.

Test Tip

It is important to remember that mass number (the total number of nuclear particles) and the charge number is conserved in radioactive decay. All the neutrons and protons should be accounted for in the equations.

D. An unstable nucleus will emit radiation depending on the type of instability it has.

1. If the neutron/proton ratio is too high, it will typically experience beta decay, in which a neutron becomes a proton and an electron and an electron antineutrino. Due to its high energy, the electron ejected from the nucleus is the *negative beta emission*.

$$_Z^A X \rightarrow _{Z+1}^A X + _{-1}^0 e + _0^0 \bar{v}_e$$

2. If the neutron/proton ratio is too low, it will typically experience positive beta decay, in which a proton becomes a neutron and a positron and an electron neutrino. Due to its high energy, the positron ejected from the nucleus is the *positive beta emission*.

$$_Z^A X \rightarrow _{Z-1}^A X + _{+1}^0 \bar{e} + _0^0 v_e$$

3. *Electron capture* occurs in rare cases when the neutron/proton ratio is too low. In this process, an inter-shell electron combines with a proton in the nucleus and a neutron and an electron neutrino results.

$$_Z^A X + _{+1}^0 e \rightarrow _{Z-1}^A X + _0^0 v$$

4. If a larger-sized nucleus has a neutron/proton ratio that is too small, then stability can be improved through emission of a helium nucleus or *alpha particle*.

$$_Z^A X \rightarrow _{Z-2}^{A-4} Y + _2^4 He$$

5. A nucleus in an excited state can emit a photon, or *gamma ray*, when either a proton or a neutron is excited and decays to a lower energy state. The excited nucleus is usually a product of radioactive decay. An example of gamma decay is:

$$_6^{14} C \rightarrow _7^{14} N^* + _{-1}^{14} e + _3^4 \bar{v}$$

The * represents the excited state of the nucleus.

$$_7^{14} N^* \rightarrow _7^{14} N + \gamma$$

IV. BINDING ENERGY AND FISSION

A. Stable nuclei have a mass that is less than the sum of the protons and neutrons in the nucleus. The difference in mass (called the *mass defect*) is directly related to the amount of energy needed to separate the nucleus. This energy is called the *binding energy*.

$$E = (\Delta m)c^2$$

➤ B is the binding energy, *J*

➤ Δm is the difference in the mass of the nucleus and the mass of the individual particles in the nucleus, *kg*

➤ c is the speed of light in a vacuum, $\sim 3 \times 10^8 \, \frac{m}{s}$

B. *Nuclear fission* is a process by which the nucleus splits into two smaller nuclei. The amount of energy released during this process is huge compared to the energy released during the combustion of a single molecule of gas.

1. For example, when uranium is bombarded with neutrons, the nucleus is excited and splits. An example of fission reaction is:

$$^1_0 n + ^{235}_{92} U \rightarrow ^{236}_{92} U^* \rightarrow ^{141}_{56} Ba + ^{92}_{36} Kr + 3^1_0 n$$

2. The final mass of the fission products is less than the initial mass of the uranium atom and neutron. The lost mass (*mass defect*) is represented by the kinetic energy of the fission products. It can be calculated using:

$$E = | \Delta m | c^2$$

3. A typical uranium fission reaction gives off 2 or 3 neutrons, which can then be captured by neighboring uranium atoms. This process is referred to as a *chain reaction*.

4. If uncontrolled, a chain reaction can lead to a *runaway reaction*. If a runaway reaction occurs, huge amounts of energy can be released causing explosions or "meltdowns."

C. Nuclear fusion occurs when two light nuclei combine to form a more massive nucleus. For example:

$$^3_2He + ^1_0n \rightarrow ^4_2He$$

1. The new more massive nuclei has a greater binding energy per nucleon, which means it has a smaller mass than the original nuclei.

2. The mass difference appears as the energy given off in the reaction.

$$E = |\Delta m|c^2$$

PART VII

THE
EXAM

Major Concepts

I. THE BIG IDEAS

A. Throughout the curriculum for AP Physics B, there are overarching concepts that can be used to connect a variety of topics.

B. It is common to see multiple topics combined in a single free-response question.

C. Common concepts used to connect topics are: Newton's Laws and Conservation of Energy.

II. NEWTON'S LAWS

A. If $a = 0$, $v =$ constant, and $\Sigma F = 0$, and vice versa.

B. The centripetal force is provided by a force (or a component of a force) that points towards the center.

> ➤ Flat Disk/flat curve—Friction is the centripetal force.

$$F_c = f$$

$$\frac{mv^2}{r} = \mu N$$

> ➤ Orbiting bodies—Gravitational force is the centripetal force. This leads to the derivation of the orbital speed equation.

$$F_c = F_g$$

$$\frac{m_2 v^2}{r} = \frac{G m_1 m_2}{r^2}$$

➤ Magnetic field—The magnetic force on the moving charge is the centripetal force.

$$F_c = F_B$$

$$\frac{mv^2}{r} = qvB$$

C. A charged particle can be suspended in an electric field (the Millikan's oil drop experiment). The electric force balances the weight.

$$F_E = mg$$

$$qE = mg$$

D. If the electric field and the magnetic field are crossed, a charged particle can move through the fields un-deflected, which means the net force is zero.

➤ The magnetic force is balancing the electric force.

$$F_B = F_E$$

$$qvB = qE$$

 III. CONSERVATION OF ENERGY

A. In the case of an object moving with no friction through a change in height and with no other non-conservative forces doing work on the object:

$$U_o + K_o = U + K$$

$$mgh_o + \frac{1}{2}mv_o^2 = mgh + \frac{1}{2}mv^2$$

B. An object compressed on a horizontal spring is released. The spring potential energy is converted to kinetic energy, assuming there is no friction between the block and the surface.

$$U_s = K$$

$$\frac{1}{2}kx_o^2 = \frac{1}{2}mv^2$$

Note: A moving object can be stopped by a spring, in which case the kinetic energy would be converted to spring potential energy.

$$\frac{1}{2}mv_o^2 = \frac{1}{2}kx^2$$

C. A charged particle is accelerated through a potential difference. The potential difference creates an electric field which applies a force to the charged particle.

$$U_E = K$$

$$qV = \frac{1}{2}mv^2$$

1. Similarly, electrons ejected from a metal surface can be stopped by applying a potential difference with the opposite polarity.

$$\frac{1}{2}mv^2 = qV$$

D. For gases, because the temperature is a measure of the kinetic energy, the speed of the molecules increases with an increase in temperature. The internal energy is the sum of the kinetic energy of the molecules. Thus, the internal energy of the system increases.

$$T \propto K \propto U$$

1. As the speed of the molecules increases, the pressure on the sides of the container increases, or the volume of the container increases, or both. The reverse is also possible.

Mastering Multiple-Choice Questions

MULTIPLE-CHOICE QUESTIONS

A. The multiple-choice questions on the AP Physics B exam can be categorized based on the way the question is worded or how the answers appear. Recognizing the type of question can help determine what strategy is best used to answer the question.

  1. A multiple-choice question contains two parts:

    i. The stem—the question or statement

    ii. The answers—a list of answers labeled (A) through (E).

B. Generally, multiple-choice questions are either *computational* or *conceptual*.

  1. A computational question will require the application of one or more equations or manipulation of equations.

  2. A conceptual question will require the recollection of a concept, term, definition, or phenomenon.

COMPUTATIONAL QUESTIONS

A. Computational questions can be asked in a variety of ways. Commonly, computational questions may be seen in the following forms:

  1. **Graphical computational**—a graph is given in the stem and the answer is numerical. The answer will require interpreting the graph and applying the correct relationship.

Example

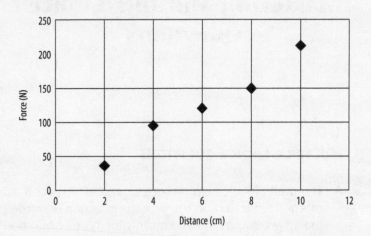

In a laboratory experiment, a student obtains the above data and displays it as a graph of the magnitude of the force applied to the spring attached to an object as a function of the stretched distance.

The force constant of the spring is most nearly

(A) $0.05 \dfrac{N}{cm}$

(B) $0.22 \dfrac{N}{cm}$

(C) $4.6 \dfrac{N}{cm}$

(D) $20 \dfrac{N}{cm}$

(E) $1100 \dfrac{N}{cm}$

Answer

In this example, the slope of the best fit straight line of a Force vs. Distance graph is the force constant, k.

With a straightedge, create a best-fit straight line. Two points from the best-fit line: (7.5, 150) and (5, 100)

$$slope = k = \frac{(150-100)}{(7.5-5)} = 20 \frac{N}{cm}$$

The correct answer is (D) $20 \frac{N}{cm}$.

Test Tip

Note the units represented on each axis—consider what the units of the slope would yield and what the units of the area would yield.

2. **Variable computational**—values, represented by variables or letters, are given in the stem and the answer is given in variables. The answer will require an equation or manipulation of equations.

Example

Planet X has a mass twice that of the Earth and a radius of one-quarter of the Earth. What is the acceleration of gravity on Planet X in terms of g, the acceleration of gravity on Earth?

(A) $\frac{g}{2}$

(B) $\frac{g}{8}$

(C) $2g$

(D) $8g$

(E) $32g$

Answer

In this example, the equation needed is the acceleration of gravity equation, $g = \frac{Gm}{r^2}$.

Using a ratio:

$$g = \dfrac{\dfrac{Gm}{r^2}}{g' = \dfrac{G(2m)}{\left(\dfrac{r}{4}\right)^2}}$$

Reducing like terms:

$$\dfrac{g = 1}{g' = \dfrac{\dfrac{1}{2}}{\left(\dfrac{1}{4}\right)^2}}$$

Which simplifies to:

$$g' = 32g$$

Where g' is the acceleration of gravity on Planet X.

The correct answer is (E) 32 g.

Test Tip

Once a correct relationship is established, substitute the variables given. If the scenario involves comparing two similar events, create a ratio of the relationships. This will allow for the elimination of common variables.

3. **Quantitative computational**—numerical values are given in the stem and the answer is also numerical. The answer will require the use of an equation or manipulation of an equation with substitution of the values to arrive at a numerical answer.

Example

A 4Ω resistor is connected to an 8 V power source. The power dissipated in the resistor is most nearly:

(A) 2 W

(B) 8 W

(C) 16 W

(D) 24 W

(E) 48 W

Answer

In this example, the resistance and voltage were given as numerical values. The power can be related to the voltage via $P = IR$. However, I is not given. Ohm's Law, $V = IR$, can be used to find the current, which can be used subsequently to find the power.

$$V = IR$$

$$8 = I4$$

$$I = 2A$$

$$P = IV$$

$$P = (2)(8)$$

$$P = 16\ W$$

The correct answer is (C) 16 W.

III. CONCEPTUAL QUESTIONS

A. Conceptual questions can be asked in a variety of ways. Conceptual questions are commonly seen in the following forms:

1. **Graphical-conceptual question**—a graph is given as part of the stem and the answers are related graphs or text that relates to the physical meaning of the graph. The answer will require applying the correct concept to the given graph and interpreting the meaning.

Example

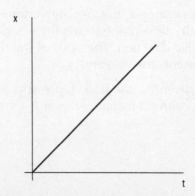

The graph on the previous page represents the velocity of an object as a function of time. Which of the following graphs of position as a function of time best represents the motion of the object?

(A)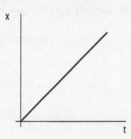

(D)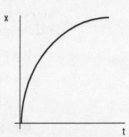

(B)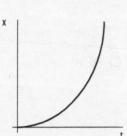

(E)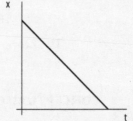

(C)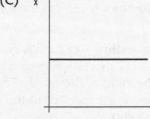

Answer

In this example, the velocity vs. time graph is given. The velocity-time graph shows the velocity increasing in the positive direction. The slope of the position vs. time graph represents the velocity.

In answer (A), the slope represents a constant velocity in the positive direction. Answer (B) shows that the slope is increasing, and represents an increasing velocity in the positive direction. Choice (C) shows that the slope is zero which represents zero velocity. In answer (D), the slope is decreasing, and represents a decreasing velocity in the positive direction. Choice (E) shows a negative slope and represents a constant velocity in the negative direction.

The correct answer is (B).

2. **Context-conceptual question**—a description of a physical situation is given in the stem and often accompanied by a diagram. The answers may be in the form of diagrams or descriptions. The answer will require applying the correct concept to the given scenario.

Example

An object is placed in front of a concave mirror. The resulting image is smaller than the object. The object must be located

(A) between the mirror and the focal point

(B) on the focal point

(C) between the focal point and the center of curvature

(D) on the center of curvature

(E) outside the center of curvature

Answer

In this example, the image created by a concave mirror is described. A quick sketch of the ray diagrams for the possible positions would be helpful in answering this question. A concave mirror creates an image smaller than the object when it is located outside the center of curvature.

The correct answer is (E).

3. **Definition-conceptual question**—a concept or the definition of a concept is identified in the stem. The answers will be given as the definition or the concept. The answer will require recollection of the concept and definition.

Example

Which of the following statements is true about the behavior of light?

    I.   light waves bend

    II. light travels though space at a constant frequency

    III. highly energetic light behaves as a particle

(A) I

(B) I and II

(C) I and III

(D) III

(E) II and III

Answer

In this example, recalling the definition of light is needed. Light exhibits wave-like and particle-like behaviors, depending on the energy of the wave. All light waves move with the same speed through a vacuum; frequency and wavelength vary.

The correct answer is (C).

IV. GENERAL STRATEGIES FOR MULTIPLE-CHOICE QUESTIONS

A. When reading a multiple-choice question, it is important to highlight the root of the question, underline important terms and circle given values or relationships.

B. Once the whole question is read, elimination of wrong answers will improve the chances of getting the correct answer.

C. Diagrams are used often. Take care in reading and interpreting diagrams for what is actually given.

D. Equations are not given during the multiple-choice section, yet success on this portion depends on correct recollection of equations.

Test Tip

Do not be fooled! You must know the equations.

E. Don't leave any answer blank. If you can't figure out an answer, try to narrow it down and then make a choice. Since the 2011 exam, there is no penalty for guessing.

Strategies for Answering Free-Response Questions

Chapter 17

I. DESIGN AND LANGUAGE OF FREE-RESPONSE QUESTIONS

A. Free-response questions are designed to test the student's ability to apply knowledge and understanding of the key concepts of physics. The stem sets up the physical situation and is followed by multiple questions (parts). The following is a list of possible directives:

> ➤ Determine the direction of specific vectors.
>
> ➤ Describe or draw the path of a particle.
>
> ➤ Draw Free-Body Diagrams.
>
> ➤ Interpret the data given.
>
> ➤ Explain the steps to solve a problem.
>
> ➤ Predict future behavior of an object or particle.
>
> ➤ Manipulate equations to yield a new relationship.
>
> ➤ Estimate values from a graph.
>
> ➤ Solve problems, numeric or symbolic, using a single equation or multiple equations.

B. Each part of a free-response question will contain a directive. Words are chosen very specifically and require students to answer in a specific manner.

1. The following list explains how the directive words should be handled.

> ➤ *Justify* and *Explain*—require the student to answer in words, equations, calculations, graphs, or diagrams. Citing laws/equations is acceptable.

➤ *Calculate*—requires that a student show all the steps of relevant work in order to receive full credit. Usually answers are numeric and require a unit.

➤ *What is* and *Determine*—does not require work, but students are strongly encouraged to show all work. Most answers are single step problems or may simply require the student to read information given on a graph.

➤ *Derive*—requires that the student begin the solution with a fundamental physics concept and show all subsequent steps that follow. Most often, students should start with an equation from the given equation sheet and the answer will be algebraic, in variable form.

➤ *Sketch*—requires that the student draw a trend for the relationship, obeying asymptotic behaviors, considering slope, intercepts, and curvature.

➤ *Plot*—requires that the student use numerical, or symbolic, values to label relevant points. The scale of the axis must be consistent for each axis and each axis should be labeled properly (quantity and unit).

2. If reference is made to a specific principle or law, such as Pascal's Principle or Hooke's Law, further explanation of the law/equation is not necessary. Students are expected to describe how the law/equation is applicable.

II. TYPES OF FREE-RESPONSE QUESTIONS

A. **Computational questions**—students are required to solve a series of questions related to the situation introduced in the stem.

1. Numeric computational problems will have numbers that will need to be substituted into the proper equations. Showing all work is imperative.

    i.   Generally, if an incorrect value is obtained and needed for subsequent sections, credit is still awarded for the correct work done with the wrong value.

    ii. Numeric answers include the unit.

2. Symbolic computational problems will have symbols defined in the stem that are to be used in the answer.

    i.   The question will ask for the answer in terms of specific variables. It is essential that the student present the final answer in terms of the symbols required.

    ii. Units are not necessary for symbolic answers as the extra notation becomes difficult to distinguish from the answer.

B. Lab-based questions—students are required to design an experiment and describe what measurements will be taken with the equipment provided and how the measurements will be used.

1. Clearly and concisely, describe the procedure. This can be done as a list of steps.

2. Describe in detail how each instrument would be used.

3. Draw a diagram and label each component.

4. Describe how the dependent variable will change if part of the experiment is altered (i.e., how does the volume of the fluid displaced change if the density of the fluid is increased?).

C. Graphing questions—students are given data and must create a graph to express a specific relationship.

1. Students must determine the relationship and how to graph the data such that the slope returns the desired quantity. Many times students must *linearize* the graph.

Example

The position of a dropped object as it is in free-fall is given with corresponding times.

Time (s)	0.2	0.3	0.4	0.5	0.6	0.7	0.8	0.9
Vertical Position (m)	−0.2	−0.4	−0.8	−1	−1.9	−2.3	−3	−3.8

The student is asked to solve for the acceleration of the object. The position vs. time gives a parabolic relationship, as shown in Figure 17.1. This does not allow the student to solve for the acceleration.

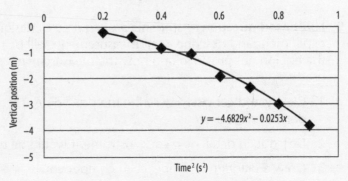

Figure 17.1

The acceleration can be related to change in position by:

$$\Delta x = v_o t + \frac{1}{2} a t^2$$

if the initial velocity is zero (dropped):

$$\Delta x = \frac{1}{2} a t^2$$

which shows that the change in position is directly related to the time squared. Therefore, by squaring the time, and plotting position vs. time squared, the line is straight, as shown in Figure 17.2. This results in a slope that is easily determined.

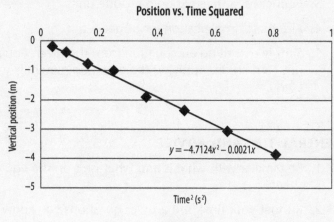

Figure 17.2

However, according to the equation, the slope would be $\frac{1}{2}a$. This final step is key in demonstrating the student's full knowledge and understanding of the problem.

> ➤ The axis must be labeled with the variable symbol or name and the unit.

> ➤ The axis must be scaled properly; each axis must have a consistent scale.

D. **Derivation questions**—students are required to start with basic equations, usually from the equation sheet, and derive a relationship from the manipulation of those equations.

1. Use symbols given in the stem.

2. Show all steps clearly.

III. GENERAL STRATEGIES FOR FREE-RESPONSE QUESTIONS

1. Scores are based on the quality of the response. Students *must show all work*.

2. Partial credit is often awarded for correct work. However, a correct answer with *insufficient* work will not receive full credit.

3. Numerical answers should include units.

4. Algebraic simplification is not needed.

5. Simply re-writing an equation from the given equations will not earn credit. Applying the equation generally will earn credit.

 GENERAL TIPS AND ADVICE

1. Be familiar with what is and what isn't on the equation sheet.

2. Budget your time and answer questions you know first.

3. Answer the question that is asked.

4. Write legibly. If the Readers can't read it, they can't score it.

5. For symbolic answers, use the symbols given, not your own.

6. If you're not sure of the answer for part (a) but you need it for part (b), make up something and follow through with the substitution.

7. When asked to justify or explain, write in complete sentences.

8. If you scratch out or erase your work, it will not be examined.

9. Putting down a wrong answer in addition to a correct answer most likely will negate the points earned for a correct answer.

10. Leave nothing to the imagination.

11. Put your answer in the space provided. If you need more space, clearly indicate where the extra work is.

12. SHOW YOUR WORK.

Essential Equations

Equation	Description
$\lvert v \rvert = \dfrac{d}{t}$	Average speed
$v = v_o + at$ $\Delta x = v_o t + \dfrac{1}{2} at^2$ $v^2 = v_o^2 + 2a\Delta x$	Kinematics equations for constant acceleration
$\Sigma F = ma$	Newton's 2nd Law
$f \leq \mu n$	Friction
$F_c = \dfrac{mv^2}{r}$	Centripetal force
$F_g = \left\lvert \dfrac{Gm_1 m_2}{r^2} \right\rvert$	Gravitational force
$F = -kx$	Hooke's Law
$W = Fd \cos \theta$	Work
$W = \Delta K$	Work-Energy theorem
$U = mgh$	Gravitational potential energy
$K = \dfrac{1}{2} mv^2$	Kinetic energy
$W_{nc} = \Delta K + \Delta U$	Conservation of energy
$U_s = \dfrac{1}{2} kx^2$	Spring potential energy
$U_g = -\dfrac{Gm_1 m_2}{r}$	Gravitational potential energy (Planets)

Equation	Description
$T_p = 2\pi\sqrt{\dfrac{L}{g}}$	Period of a pendulum
$T_s = 2\pi\sqrt{\dfrac{m}{k}}$	Period of a spring
$v = \dfrac{2\pi r}{T}$	Tangential speed
$P = \dfrac{W}{t} = Fv$	Power
$p = mv$	Momentum
$m_1 v_{1_0} + m_2 v_{2_0} = m_1 v_1 + m_2 v_2$	Conservation of momentum
$J = \Delta p = F\Delta t$	Impulse-momentum theorem
$P = \dfrac{F}{A}$	Pressure
$P = P_o + \rho g h$	Absolute pressure
$\rho = \dfrac{m}{V}$	Density
$A_1 v_1 = A_2 v_2$	Continuity equation
$P_1 + \dfrac{1}{2}\rho v_1^2 + \rho g h_1 = P_2 + \dfrac{1}{2}\rho v_2^2 + \rho g h_2$	Bernoulli's equation
$PV = nRT$	Ideal Gas Law equation
$\Delta U = Q + W$	First Law of Thermodynamics
$\Delta L = \propto L_o \Delta T$	Length expansion
$H = \dfrac{kA\Delta T}{L}$	Heat transfer

Equation	Description
$v = f\lambda$	Speed of a wave
$f = \dfrac{1}{T}$	Frequency
$f_n = \dfrac{nv}{2L}$	Frequency of nth harmonic on a string/ Frequency of wave in open/open pipe
$v = \sqrt{\dfrac{T}{\frac{m}{l}}}$	Speed of a wave on a string
$f_n = \dfrac{nv}{4L}$	Frequency of nth harmonic in open/closed pipe
$F = \dfrac{kq_1q_2}{r^2}$	Coulomb's Law
$E = \dfrac{kQ}{r^2}$	Electric field of a charge
$U_E = \dfrac{kq_1q_2}{r}$	Electric potential energy between two charges
$V = \dfrac{kQ}{r}$	Electric potential of a charge
$F = qE$	Force on a charge in E field
$U = qV$	Potential energy of a charge at a given potential
$V = Ed$	Potential difference across a uniform E field
$V = IR$	Ohm's Law
$R = \dfrac{\rho L}{A}$	Resistance of a conductor
$I = \dfrac{Q}{t}$	Current
$P = IV = I^2R = \dfrac{V^2}{R}$	Power

Equation	Description
$R_s = R_1 + R_2 + \ldots$	Resistors in series
$\dfrac{1}{R_p} = \dfrac{1}{R_1} + \dfrac{1}{R_2} + \ldots$	Resistors in parallel
$Q = CV$	Charge on a capacitor
$C = \varepsilon_0 \dfrac{A}{d}$	Capacitance
$U_c = \dfrac{1}{2}CV^2 = \dfrac{1}{2}QV$	Energy stored in a capacitor
$\dfrac{1}{C_s} = \dfrac{1}{C_1} + \dfrac{1}{C_2} + \ldots$	Capacitors in series
$C_p = C_1 + C_2 + \ldots$	Capacitors in parallel
$F_B = qvB \sin \theta$	Magnetic force equation
$B = \dfrac{\mu_0 I}{2\pi r}$	Magnetic field of a long straight wire
$F_B = I\ell B \sin \theta$	Magnetic force on a current carrying wire
$\dfrac{F}{\ell} = \dfrac{\mu_0 I_1 I_2}{2\pi d}$	Force between two current carrying wires
$\Phi = BA \cos \theta$	Magnetic flux
$\varepsilon = \dfrac{\Delta \Phi}{\Delta t}$	Induced emf (Faraday's Law)
$\varepsilon = B\ell v$	Motional emf
$Tan\, \theta = \dfrac{y}{L}$	Double slit
$d \sin \theta = m\lambda$	Double slit max, single slit min
$E = mc^2$	Energy-mass equation
$E = hf = \dfrac{hc}{\lambda}$	Energy of a photon

Equation	Description
$K = hf - \Phi$	Kinetic energy of ejected electron
$n = \dfrac{c}{v}$	Index of refraction
$n_1 \sin \theta_1 = n_2 \sin \theta_2$	Snell's Law
$\theta_c = \sin \dfrac{n_2}{n_1}$	Critical angle
$f = \dfrac{R}{2}$	Mirror focal point
$\dfrac{1}{s_o} + \dfrac{1}{s_i} = \dfrac{1}{f}$	Mirror equation/thin lens equation
$M = \dfrac{s_i}{s_o} = \dfrac{-h_i}{h_o}$	Magnification

Notes

Notes

Notes

Notes